Dream Home

D1313943

WITHDRAWN
FROM THE RODMAN PUBLIC LIBRARY

INNERFORMSLTD.COM

This is the special economical edition of Dream Home, with text and images printed in black and white. For the full-color deluxe edition, consider buying your copy from www.dreamhomethebook.com, and from either www.amazon.com or www.barnesandnoble.com under Alofsin Dream Home. The content of the text is the same for both editions.

Dream Home

What You Need to Know Before You Buy

Dr. Anthony Alofsin, AIA

RODMAN PUBLIC LIBRARY

38212002980354
Main Adult
643.12 A453
Alofsin, Anthony
Dream home

Book jacket: designed by Jeanie Fan
Author photo: Ben Collier, Photographer

First CreateSpace paperback black and white edition.
© 2013 Anthony Alofsin. All rights reserved. No part of this publication may be reproduced in any form without written permission from Innerformsltd.com.

ISBN-13: 978-1484802151

Please post your comments about Dream Home and see the latest discussion and research on home buying at www.dreamhomethebook.com

Table of Contents

7   **Introduction: A Few Words Before You Buy**

17   **Part I: The Players**
17   The Buyers
21   The Marketers
24   Big Builders
27   Local Builders and Contractors
27   Plan Factories
30   Developers
36   Media

39   **Part II: The Visit**
39   Preparations
46   Case Study 1: Fairway Estates
55   Façades
59   The Overall Experience
72   Case Study 2: Rose Hill
77   The Purchase Process

81   **Part III: A Closer Look**
81   Siting
86   Space and Proportions
91   Custom Design
92   The Same But Different

99   **Part IV: What's in a Name?**
99   Styles: A Brief History of Architecture
109   The Styles Adapted to Housing: Then versus Now
128   Minimal Cues
130   Names and Themes

141   **Conclusion**

145   **Sources**

149   **Notes**

150   **Acknowledgments**

150   **Credits**

Real Estate

This house at 18410 Crosstimber St. is in Rogers Ranch, a neighborhood attractive to Mexicans. At 3,600 square feet, it lists for $399,900.

SPACES

Lisa Krantz / San Antonio Express-News

Rental's a real gem

An apartment at the Pearl Brewery smack in the middle of a parade of activities. **Page D5**

MARKETING

Patterns emerge in Mexicans' purchases

North S.A. a destination for many

By David Hendricks

When Mexicans shop for houses in San Antonio, either to live in permanently or as a second home, they like to live close to other Mexicans who have chosen San Antonio as their U.S. city.

"They feel more comfortable," said Cora Turpin, a real estate agent for Keller Williams Legacy Group Realty. "They also like to be near businesses that belong to Mexicans."

Some prime areas where Mexicans are congregating in San Antonio are in Stone Oak, especially the Sonterra section, Rogers Ranch and the Dominion, said Turpin, who specializes in serving Mexicans looking for residential real estate.

Some Mexicans are exceptions, however, said Jean Marie Ruffini, an agent with Coldwell Banker D'Ann Harper Realtors' Northwest office. A few have been looking and buying in the Elm Creek, Alon and Whispering Oaks areas to be closer to the central city, Ruffini said.

"They may prefer to live in North Central inside Loop 1604 where they would be closer to the Medical Center, airport, the University of Texas at San Antonio, USAA, Hardberger Park and the new Alon shopping center," Ruffini said. "The driving congestion and the construction at the intersection of (U.S.) 281 and 1604 may begin to take the bloom off of the Sonterra area."

More than 50,000 San Antonio residences are owned by Mexicans, said lawyer Robert Braubach.

About 10 percent of the houses in Northwest San Antonio are owned by Mexicans, especially houses in gated, secure subdivisions, Braubach said.

In Sonterra, Mexicans are buying houses from the upper $200,000 to $500,000 range, Turpin said.

Some Mexicans prefer Rogers Ranch because it

Mexicans continues on D6

This bedroom in a Whispering Oaks subdivision home is airy and bright, an ambience that Mexican home buyers like, real estate agents say.

This house at 2003 My Anns Hill in the Big Springs subdivision is in an area also favored by Mexicans. At 4,282 square feet, it is listed at $810,000.

BUY MY HOUSE!
PAID ADVERTISING

The house sits on one acre with mature oak trees, expensive views of the Hill Country and a full outdoor kitchen.

House built for Parade of Homes has lots of extras

PROPERTY: Two-story home built in 2010 in the Copper Ridge subdivision by David Mills Custom Homes

ADDRESS: 331 Copper Crest, New Braunfels, 78132

SIZE: 4,318 sq. ft., 4 bedrooms, 4.5 baths

LIST PRICE: $874,900

CONTACT INFORMATION: David Mills, (210) 618-3127, davidmills@davidmillscustomhomes.com

MLS NUMBER: 931145

The homeowner's story:

HOW LONG HAS THE HOUSE BEEN ON THE MARKET? Two years.

WHY DO YOU THINK NO ONE HAS SNAPPED IT UP? There are not many people in the New Braunfels area who are looking for a home in this price range in the current economy.

How to submit:
Want to stand out in a buyer's market? Is there something exciting and unique about your house? Then let us help you!

For pricing and information, call (210) 250-2309 or e-mail emann@express-news.net.

WHAT ARE SOME OF THE TOP FEATURES OF THE HOUSE? The home was built for a Parade of Homes that never happened, so there are a lot of extra features you won't normally find in a model home. San Antonio's John Moss designed the house. As the first home in the neighborhood, it was cool to see this vacant piece of land and the house go up with nothing around it for miles.

BUY continues on D4

HIGHLIGHTS: When vibrant landscaping pops against colorful exteriors, you get homes like these!

Courtesy photo

Loop 1604 and Military Drive West

Location: Highpoint at Westcreek, 715 Point Sunset
Size: About 2,575 sq. ft., 4 beds, 3½ baths
Amenities: Open floor plan, game room, island kitchen, Corian counters, formal dining, hardwoods, master suite down, fireplace, backyard fire pit, special yard lighting, comm. clubhouse, pool, sports court, jogging trails
List price: $199,990
Contact Information: Re/Max North-San Antonio, Sandra Rangel, 210-334-7717
MLS number: 944689

Courtesy photo

Universal City

Location: Olympia, 8602 Mount Latmos
Size: About 2,977 sq. ft., 4 beds, 3½ baths
Amenities: Corner lot, mature trees, 2-story pillared entrance, game room, master suite down w/sitting area, garden tub, dual vanity, formal dining, island kitchen w/ cook top, built-ins, French doors, sprinkler system, patio
List price: $235,000
Contact Information: Phyllis Browning Co., Debbie Garza, 210-325-5696
MLS number: 942344

Courtesy photo

Huebner and Bitters roads

Location: Huebner Village, 2506 Huebner Park
Size: About 2,040 sq. ft., 3 beds, 2½ baths
Amenities: In cul-de-sac, all stucco, tile roof, open floor plan, gas cooking, stone breakfast bar, mature palm tree, granite counters, stainless steel appliances, master w/ outside access, garden tub, covered back porch
List price: $320,000
Contact Information: Keller Williams Realty, The Boehm Team, Amy Boehm, 830-428-8106
MLS number: 936762

To suggest a listing for this space, e-mail realestate@express-news.net. For more information and photos, enter the MLS number at mySA.com/realestate

---

Figs. 1 and 2: Real estate section, *San Antonio Express-News.*

INTRODUCTION

A Few Words Before You Buy

You're considering buying a home. You might begin by looking at the listings in real estate websites and in the Sunday real estate section of your local newspaper (Figs. 1-2). When looking at the homes pictured there, do you wonder where the designs come from, who made them, and who is marketing them? Do you know whether you will be getting value for your money? Do you ask yourself whether these homes really fit your needs and desires? *Dream Home* explores these questions explicitly for people looking to buy either a newly constructed or a yet-to-be constructed house. It guides you toward getting the home of your dreams. This book gives you the information, knowledge, and tools to be an informed consumer. If you can articulate what you need and want, the building industry will respond positively. As part of its standard practice, the housing industry alters the design of homes in response to buyer demand, and increasingly it relies on marketing surveys and consumer profiles to find what appeals to customers. The industry will listen to you—it wants to give you what you want.

A home, in addition to being a major financial investment, is a primary means of expressing personal identity. A home says something about the people who live in it, and the kind of people who live in their own homes has evolved over the last seventy years. In the mid-1940s, the mass-production housing industry was

Fig. 2

just getting off the ground, and it built homes primarily for returning World War II veterans who were starting families. Today, it builds homes for the middle class, the upper middle class, and even the very rich. During those same seventy years, the American family has changed dramatically. The traditional family of father, mother, and three children, although still prevalent, is not the only family structure. Besides the traditional family, the housing market today builds homes for singles, couples without children, families with older children living at home, and those needing accommodations for in-laws or aging parents. Demographics show that the United States is becoming ever more diverse, and the housing industry is learning to address the needs of a variety of ethnic and cultural groups. No longer is the industry mostly geared toward preferences of the white middle class.

Despite the lingering effects of the recession that hit in 2008, the housing industry is regaining its role as a major component of U.S. economic strength. If you are interested in buying a home or having one built for you, now is the best time to prepare yourself to make your dreams a reality.

The more you understand about the housing industry and the homes it provides, the better equipped you will be to find the home that's right for you. Note that *Dream Home*'s emphasis is on new construction—finding and evaluating previously occupied houses is not its focus. The book has four parts to help you achieve your goals.

Part I introduces you to **The Players**—real estate agents and home builders. It demystifies the terms and jargon used by the housing industry. It takes you on a visit to a suburban housing development and educates you about the houses you see there. It explains what is involved in choosing and purchasing a home and its finishes. We also look at the important roles of developers and the providers of stock designs in providing the plans used for most projects.

Part II takes you on a **Visit** to a typical model home. You will experience its neighborhood and its location on the way to the site, then look in detail at a typical model home and the design choices you can expect to be offered. We go on the typical journey any home buyer would experience in preparing to shop for a home, visiting model homes at a builder's site and then following through to purchase a new residence. It should be noted that model homes come in all styles and are targeted to virtually all income levels, so the questions that buyers face in this situation are similar regardless of the house's price. The visit then moves to the design

TERMS

A few helpful definitions.

Custom Design as used in the building industry, the term applies to a standard tract house that is personalized according to your own taste and choices. Custom design means something different from a unique house conceived by an architect or home designer.

Home the house that you personally identify with as your special place.

House a generic product of the construction industry. There is a difference between a house and a home: a house, an object of consumption, feels transient, regardless of how long people live in it; a home is a place of comfort and refuge that we imagine is solid and long lasting.

House Building Industry the commercial business interests that buy property, construct houses, and sell them. The building industry produces large numbers of houses by means of mass production, similar to how automobiles are produced. The industry's methods of building and marketing are relatively similar whether the house is small, medium, or large in size. Prices and marketing approaches are adjusted, however, for the location of a subdivision, the size of lots, and the size of houses.

Subdivision a large tract of land that has been parceled into smaller, individual lots. Some subdivisions may have amenities such as parks, open spaces, and shared facilities; others may not. Usually, subdivisions are created by developers and house building companies. They can range from groups of just a few houses to large-scale tracts requiring years to develop.

Tract House the typical house found in a subdivision.

center, where you select the finishes for your home; it may be eye-opening to see how these choices will have a huge impact on the final cost of your project.

Part III—**A Closer Look**—considers the importance of siting, proportions, and orientation, particularly their impact on your utility costs, comfort, and sense of well-being. This discussion takes in the idea of "custom design," a term that is about a carefully controlled range of detail options and finishes, not a unique design. A fundamental practice in the housing industry emerges here: the same designs are circulated throughout the country, but their names are changed, and prices adjusted, depending on location and demand. It may come as surprise to learn that a "custom" home is neither unique nor custom. To help you be effective in comparing the "custom" options you can expect to be offered, some of the conventions that describe architectural designs—terms such as plan, elevation, and section—are defined. Getting a handle on this terminology will allow you to talk clearly about homes and what you want in one.

Part IV—**What's in a Name?**—talks about the styles of houses, what they used to look like and what they look like now. This might seem like school lessons or even technical, but nowhere else can you find these subjects discussed. And a sense of understanding where these styles came from tells you where your own home came from. This section also discusses the concept of style as it applies to fashion and to architecture. In the past, for people who could afford to build, styles had specific associations and clear distinctions that could be grasped and described. Now, the styles' meanings are no longer obvious and they are unrecognizable. **Themes** and general categories, like Traditional, European, Mediterranean, and Tuscan, have replaced the old, standard styles and their revivals. These themes do affect, even if subtly, our perception of our homes and neighborhoods. The styles no longer mean what they once did.

The **Conclusion** looks at the some of the broad and important ways a house represents who you are and how you can be well prepared to express your identity and values in your home. It ends with a summary of the four key points you need to follow in order to be a better-informed consumer. A section on helpful **Sources** of more information concludes the book.

Most people are unfamiliar with the workings of the building industry, and they have only a general awareness of their buildings as architecture. You might know something about the human body from studying biology in school, but few people

Fig. 3: François de Menil Residence, Gwathmey, Siegel, Kaufman & Associates Architects, East Hampton, New York, 1983. © Norman McGrath

ever study architecture. What people do know about architecture comes from the experience of where and how they grew up, anything they may have learned from their families, and from images seen in print magazines, television, photographs, and the Internet. For most people, the subject of architecture is perplexing, and the connection between formal architecture and their homes can seem obscure. Nonetheless, architecture subtly (or not) affects our **taste** for the kinds of buildings we find appealing (or not). Taste is difficult to define and problematic to judge. But being aware of your own taste can help ensure that the home you buy closely matches your dream home.

Nostalgia, the human tendency to yearn for an imagined time or a past place, is a definite factor in taste. Some people scorn nostalgia, seeing it as a means of avoiding the present and all its complications. But nostalgia can be a way to connect with our roots and traditions and the foundations of who we are. It may help us create a world that comforts and supports our families and ourselves. Unsurprisingly, nostalgia plays a major role in the housing industry. For example, despite some people's interest in flat-roofed modernist houses with a great deal of glass and a lack of traditional details, the majority of American home buyers still prefer pitched-roofed homes with traditional associations (Fig. 3). Beyond nostalgia, **marketing** also affects Americans' preference for a pitched-roof house. It is the style of house most readily available, most reasonably priced, and, we are told, most suitable for our lifestyles.

At the beginning of the twenty-first century, in the most technologically advanced conditions the world has seen, a large percentage of houses are still based on architectural images whose origins go back to traditions hundreds of years old. Some people might argue that old styles have the benefit of a track record. No style is better than another—Tuscan, for example, is not better than modernist, or vice versa—but the clear expression of style is a real factor in the quality of a home. Does the design of a house complement the way you live or how you want to live? A successful home is one that communicates integrity, provides for its owners' needs, and shows sensitivity to its site, regardless of its style.

A preference for a pitched-roof house over a flat-roof house still dominates, however, in people's choices. The pitched-roof house communicates "home" in clear and familiar ways, and those qualities are comforting and reassuring. This image, which is rooted in the American psyche, began with the first shelters created by the earliest settlers and continues to the present. Sketches by the cartoonist Comfort Thresher show with clarity the basic exterior features of a home (Figs. 4 - 5). His site is in Glendale, California, but it could be almost anywhere. Our eye immediately focuses on three elements: the **pitched roof, dormered windows** (a protrusion from a sloping roof), and a **fanlight** (a window located above the front door). These elements from the past are so basic, so pervasive in the present that they have become fundamental in thinking about the American home. People's memories and associations of childhood identify these fundamental elements with the home. A pitched roof, dormers, and a clearly visible doorway signify home; whereas a flat roof, irregular windows, and an obscured entry mean something else: an office, a factory, or the anti-home.

It is no wonder that purchasing a home is a daunting task, particularly for first-time buyers. In addition to the traditional sources of information—newspapers, magazines, and books—that can help with your preparation, an explosion of digital media now piles on information. Numerous programs on network and cable television expand buyers' awareness of home styles, interiors, building practices, even landscaping and gardening. The Internet successfully competes with print media and television as a means of marketing houses. And national builders are taking full advantage of this tool, allowing you to virtually compose your dream home online. A typical website for a major builder of high-end tract houses shows how effective interactive digital communication can be. For starters, you can pick any city to search in the regions the company serves. From there, you may have the opportunity to assemble your own design. After selecting the number of bedrooms, bathrooms, and garages you want, you immediately get the preexisting models, along with their sizes in square feet, that fit your requirements. You then get to choose the façade (front) of your house from a set of options, along with design and finish choices. This kind of fluid flexibility and immediacy has no precedent in the age-old process of building a home. With amazing rapidity, you can have a picture of your dream home. A savvy national builder looking to target a particular market and audience might even include a brochure in Spanish, Chinese, Korean, Vietnamese, or any one of a dozen languages.

The use of the Internet will become an increasingly powerful means of choosing, buying, and selling real estate. Websites such as Realtor.com, Trulia.com, and Zillow.com are just the beginning. Ironically, sometimes instead of making consumers' choices easier, the Internet overwhelms them with options. What gets lost in the proliferation of images of houses and plans and fixtures is a deeper discussion about ideas of beauty, what homes mean, and how they communicate that meaning. The presence of beauty is important. Without it, our lives are diminished. You can have an efficient, properly sited, and technologically innovative house that is also beautiful. Consequently, it makes sense to take some time to think about what you want and what you are getting when you pursue your dream home. Pause before buying—it's a smart thing to do. Buyers should also consider the resale value of their homes, keeping in mind that future homebuyers will likely be looking for quality over square footage, and energy efficiency over features.

As we consider the steps necessary to put you in your dream home, I will be your guide and assistant, explaining how the home building industry operates, analyzing its products for you, preparing you for the multitude of decisions facing you, and encouraging you on your journey. As a practicing architect and an architectural historian who has written many books and articles about Frank Lloyd Wright and modern architecture, I have long been interested in what kind of housing

Figs. 4 - 5: Glendale Memories, C. Thresher, 1986.

Americans get when they purchase their homes. I have built my own home and steered clients through their own home-building processes, so I know personally how you feel when confronting the huge number of questions that come up and the resulting stress and anxiety that the process may induce. We are in this exploration together, so whenever I use the word "we" in this book, I mean you and me. Hopefully, after reading *Dream Home* you will be a more informed—and more confident—consumer when you enter the market for a new home. May your dream home become a reality.

-- Anthony Alofsin, AIA 🏠

Text Color Keys   IMPORTANT TERMS

KEY CONCEPTS

PART I

The Players

THE BUYERS

Who are the players in this marketplace of homes? There are **buyers,** which means you, the domestic consumer. There are **marketers,** whose role is to sell and transact the exchange of goods and services. The **builders** or **contractors,** both small and large, provide the houses for buyers. There are also several sub-industries that support the system but are largely invisible to the public. They include national trade organizations, materials suppliers, companies that specialize in providing stock designs, and media outlets.

You are the consumer and you know your particular tastes and needs, but the building industry relies on broad profiles to target its markets. The profiles of generic buyers today are more complex than they were fifty years ago. Conventional ideas about the size of a family (two adults and three children) have given way to smaller numbers of children (and maybe only one parent), as well as unconventional arrangements of partners, lifelong singles, people marrying at older ages, and the tides of baby boomers now entering retirement. The housing industry has an obvious interest in defining its potential clients, and it conducts detailed studies of likely buyers. Few industries are more sensitive to the needs and desires—and vulnerabilities—of its potential consumers.

In July 2012, *Professional Builder,* a major trade journal, published the results of a survey that asked 20,000 potential buyers about design issues. When asked about the most important characteristics when buying their next home, almost 60 percent of respondents indicated that home design was as important as location. Safety followed closely behind. Price came in fourth place (55 percent), followed by community design and accessibility. The least important factor was prestige: only 13 percent of respondents said it was important (Fig. 6). With respect to specific rooms

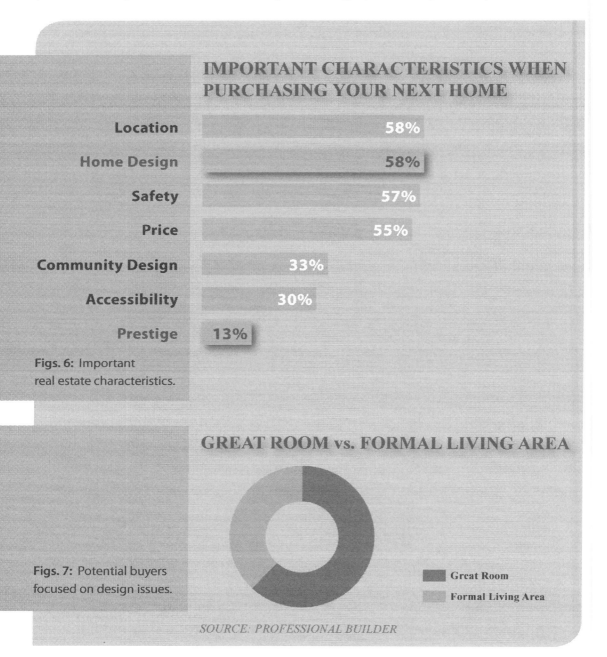

IMPORTANT CHARACTERISTICS WHEN PURCHASING YOUR NEXT HOME

Location	58%
Home Design	58%
Safety	57%
Price	55%
Community Design	33%
Accessibility	30%
Prestige	13%

Figs. 6: Important real estate characteristics.

GREAT ROOM vs. FORMAL LIVING AREA

Figs. 7: Potential buyers focused on design issues.

Great Room
Formal Living Area

SOURCE: PROFESSIONAL BUILDER

in a house, buyers were asked whether they preferred a great room or a formal area. The great room, an expanded den turned into an open family room, trounced the formal living area, 62 to 38 percent. Formal spaces were seen as privileged spaces for more affluent buyers (Fig. 7).

Other points that emerged in this survey on design preferences:

- House designs should start from the inside and work out, particularly for people with children. The role of social spaces, inside or out, was seen as critical.

- Great home design need not cost the builder more than mediocre design.

- Outdoor space has more than entertainment value; buyers see it as an important buffer of privacy between neighbors.

- Connections between indoor and outdoor spaces are a must.

- Buyers prefer a casual look.

- Most buyers do not really want urban living. Suburban and detached homes are still preferred by all age groups. But Generation Ys (roughly, those born from 1980 to 2000) without children are more likely to pick attached or rental houses close to their jobs. Married people with children have different preferences.

- Interest in "contemporary" interior styling has risen dramatically. Contemporary exteriors are still at the bottom of preference lists, but people are becoming more interested in "clean lines" and a "contemporary feel." This preference is reflected in Pottery Barn being the most popular home furnishings retailer in 2011. Crate and Barrel and even Ethan Allan, a company long associated with traditional taste, are adding contemporary lines. This trend may be seen in the increasing availability of contemporary-style cabinetry, faucets, fixtures, and sinks.

The diversifying U.S. population will have a big impact on the industry and the homes it builds. A few figures underlie this trend. In 2010, whites made up 63.7 percent of the population. But Hispanics accounted for 55.5 percent of U.S. population growth from 2000 to 2010, compared to 8.3 percent for whites . These figures mean the Hispanic population will become increasing important in every aspect of America life—as will Asian communities, which also showed impressive growth rates over the last decade, through immigration as well as births. Other studies indicate that seven out of ten new households will be formed by minorities. The days of baby boomers as the primary home buyers will change as more of them retire. Married couples are now a minority as heads of families. And baby boomers are less mobile than younger Americans; people in their twenties are eight times more likely than boomers to move, and the economic downturn has kept many of the older generation in place.

Going from general categories to more concrete pictures, the industry benefits from "psychographic" market research. These are studies that try to define the psychological profiles of prominent buyer groups. For example, the **National Association of Home Builders (NAHB),** the major professional organization of the building industry, keeps itself informed about consumers' wants and needs. At its January 2011 meeting in Orlando, Florida, attended by 47,000 people, the NAHB surveyed the industry by getting feedback from 238 builders, manufacturers, designers, and architects on what buyers want. The respondents pointed to compact, energy-efficient, affordable houses situated on smaller lots near walking trails and open spaces. These trends reflect what consumers themselves want: smaller homes, in part because empty nesters are seeking energy-efficient dwellings. The Economics and Housing Policy Group, a professional survey company, reported at the meeting that by 2015 the average size of the new house will be 2,000–2,399 square feet, versus the current size of 2,500 square feet. The living room will disappear as it merges into another living space.

The findings from the NAHB meeting further confirm that builders are highly aware of their consumers' priorities: because we still have enough income to acquire more stuff, more storage is necessary; we still have time for leisure activities that require space; and energy consciousness is deepening as a fact of everyday life for most consumers. In other words, despite an economic downturn, political anxiety, a polarized populace, and global unrest, Americans still have a good life, and the housing industry will continue to shelter us.

Something is missing, however, from the survey findings in *Professional Builder* and from the NAHB meeting: discussions about the styles of homes. Although "design" was of special interest in the magazine survey, the topic referred to spaces within a house and how people use them. In other words, design was treated as the equivalent of a building program corresponding to a client's desires. Consumers want relaxed and informal atmospheres, but their preferences for one style over another are not apparent. What a house looks like is far less important than consumers' specific needs and desires. The significance of this trend is twofold: either what houses look like has become irrelevant, or the image of a house has a meaning that operates at a vague, unconscious level.

It pays to remember that you as the buyer are the subject of the building industry's nearly constant process of surveying your wants and needs. As a result, you may be more powerful in influencing your housing choices than you realize.

THE MARKETERS

We've looked a bit at the buyer as revealed by national surveys. Now let's look at the marketer, a central player in the home-buying process. There are two types of professionals whose job is to sell you a house: an independent **real estate agent** and a **marketing person** who works for a building company or contractor. First, we will look at the real estate agent, the facilitator of deals between buyers and sellers. Real estate agents may represent either buyer or seller—an important distinction—and they receive a percentage of the sale price in commission.

Approximately two million men and women work in the United States as real estate agents, but less than half may be continually active. Real estate agents are licensed by the states where they work, and they must work for a broker. Many people use the term "realtor" as a synonym of "real estate agent," but in fact "Realtor" is the trademarked designation of an agent who is a member of the **National Association of Realtors (NAR)** and subscribes to its code of ethics, commits to continuing education, and has access to professional resources. About half of the two million active real estate licensees in the United States are Realtors. The NAR provides its members with a broad range of services, including research, blogs, marketing tips, information for interested buyers, and, through its political action committee, lobbying. The NAR offers training designed to expand its members' expertise. Real estate **brokers** have more training and education than agents and have a broker's license, which is required to sell real estate in an office or corporate firm.

Typically, states require prospective real estate agents to take courses in principles of real estate, laws of agency, laws of contracts, and related courses. After fulfilling the education requirement, the applicant takes a licensing exam. Other requirements may include arranging for a licensed broker to provide sponsorship, undergoing background checks, and, recently, being fingerprinted.

While the educational and licensing process helps prevent just anyone from arbitrarily claiming the ability to be a real estate agent, certification emphasizes the legal and procedural aspects of the profession. Agents, Realtors, and brokers are not required to have any knowledge of architectural history, style, design aesthetics, or practical issues such as siting or energy requirements. Some information of this sort can be gleaned from others sources—the Realtor.org website has a section on home styles, presumably as a resource for Realtors—but expertise in this area is not mandatory.

The real estate profession is dominated by women. They account for 60 percent of Realtors, 55 percent of brokers, and 66 percent of agents. A number of real estate agents work part-time or are temporarily inactive, and in many instances they

BRIEF HISTORY

NAR

1908 Founded
National Association of
Real Estate Exchanges

1916
National Association of
Real Estate Boards

1972
National Association of
Realtors

According to its website, the National Association of Realtors was founded as the National Association of Real Estate Exchanges in 1908 in Chicago, Illinois, "to unite the real estate men of America for the purpose of effectively exerting a combined influence upon matters affecting real estate interests." Eventually, it was named the National Association of Real Estate Boards, and in 1972 received its current name. It became the largest trade association in the United States in the early 1970s and currently has over 1 million members in 54 state Associations (including Guam, Puerto Rico, and the Virgin Islands) and more than 1,400 local Associations. Among the top three states, California has the highest number of Realtors, followed by Florida and Texas. The NAR provides a broad range of services for Realtors from research to blogs to marketing tips, information for interested buyers, and, through its political action committee, advocacy for its members' interests through lobbying of governmental agencies. The NAR also provides training for designations and certifications, which expands its members' expertise. The training ranges from dealing with distressed sales to helping Realtors better serve the online needs of clients.

are balancing the demands of family with the necessity of earning a living. The nature of the profession, especially its flexible work hours, makes the job appealing.

Regardless of gender, real estate agents are middlemen. (Note: Though there are important distinctions among agents, Realtors, and brokers, as noted above, from this point on I refer to "agents" generally to mean anyone in the business of selling you a home.) They get paid for acting as an intermediary between a builder (the producer) and you, the buyer (also known as the consumer). Why not go directly to the producer to obtain the product from him and thereby save the fee? This can occur if you commission a house from a builder directly, but real estate agents justify their fees by providing valuable services to whomever they represent. Agents have access to multiple listing services, which conveniently bring together groups of properties on the market, organized by type, size, location, and asking price, along with images that range from still pictures to virtual walk-throughs. Many agents now use the Internet to market their services and to keep their clients informed. For example, some allow clients to search listings according to "lifestyle" preferences, and others include sections of market research on their websites, with monthly video presentations on real estate trends.

It is important to know whom an agent represents and how the agent's fee will be paid. If you hire an agent, you want him or her to represent your interests. Representing both a buyer and seller may pose a conflict of interest. Anybody whose job consists of collecting commissions without producing anything physically tangible might appear to be in an enviable position. And once you start looking at real estate announcements and note the photo layouts featuring elegantly dressed real estate agents, particularly those working at the high end of the market, you might assume these glamorous-looking ladies are well paid (Fig. 8). Some of them are, but real estate is a tough business. Almost 70 percent of an agent's fees are split with other agents. Competition is fierce, and the business overall is cyclically dependent on the larger economy. And the work can be frustrating: agents may spend hours or weeks or months showing properties to people who end up not purchasing a home through them.

Real estate agents may take their clients to new subdivisions to show the model homes offered by builders. There on-site, you and your agent will meet the second type of marketer: a person working for the company providing the housing. Though it may not be obvious, sometimes the building company pays the real estate agent a fee to bring you, the consumer, in as a potential sale. Salespersons working for building companies may or may not have previous experience as real estate

Fig. 8: Keller Williams Realty Company advertisement.

agents. Although they may know as much about real estate law and practice as an independent real estate agent, their job is to sell the properties offered exclusively by their company. Consequently, they have detailed information about the houses you may be considering. They are a key player in your quest to purchase an existing house or have one built for you.

BIG BUILDERS

The **National Association of Home Builders (NAHB)**, mentioned above, has over 210,000 members, one-third of them builders or remodelers, with the rest in related fields of mortgage finance, building products, and services. According to the NAHB website, in a typical year during the building boom (2003), its builders constructed 80 percent of all new housing and represented one of the largest and most powerful engines of economic growth in the country.

NAHB builders fall into three groups: **custom builders,** who build on land provided by clients, with a focus on high-end housing; **production builders,** who build twenty-five or more units a year by using industrial plans in all ranges of housing types; and **small, local production builders,** who construct fewer than twenty-five homes a year.

Even in a financial downturn, the big builders in the housing industry are major business players. As can be seen from the sidebar (page 26), the ten largest companies had combined revenues of more than $19.5 billion in 2011, when they sold almost 74,000 homes. And these figures are far lower than they were in the boom era preceding the slump in the housing market, which began in the spring of 2006. These companies, which are regionally focused, have a great deal of control over sites, material selections, and the designs of their products.

Housing is a large, profitable business. Its top executives are well paid. In a boom year like 2003, the CEOs of the three largest publicly traded housing companies were each paid $16 million to $26 million. The dozen or so largest builders—the national leaders—are publicly owned companies. Public ownership gives them ready access to capital, which allows them to take advantage of huge economies of scale and compete fiercely on price. But their investors expect a profit every quarter, which puts pressure on the companies to produce short-term results. By contrast, most home-building companies are smaller and privately owned. While privately owned companies may not have access to as much capital as large builders do for funding their projects, they don't have to meet stockholders' expectations and can plan for the long term.

Large firms have their own in-house architecture departments. These departments are divided by region, and some have as many as 100 house plans in their portfolios. The designer for the in-house architecture department provides elevation alternatives and plan options. The actual design of the house remains the same, but carefully controlled variations in the interior and exterior create the impression that the buyer is receiving a custom home. An **elevation** is a view of a building, usually from the north, south, east, or west. Elevations are what sell the houses in a subdivision and account for price variations; the interiors are almost always the same. The houses are marketed as custom homes but, in fact, are not. The options provide limited variety and yet are a large source of profit. For example, the price for a walk-up attic may be $12,000, even though it costs the builder only a couple hundred dollars, since all he has to provide is a pull-down set of stairs that leads to an unfinished attic space.

Controlling the number of options offered to consumers is critical to builders' bottom line, in large part because of a new trend: the use of long-term **warranties.** Housing companies now are responsible for warranties lasting fifteen to twenty-five years. Consequently, they are obligated to build with durable materials in order to reduce the expense of having to return and make repairs over a number of years. Sometimes this need for durability causes friction between a building company and a contractor in the field. For example, a contractor may want to use vinyl siding, which will not hold up over sustained periods of time, rather than brick or stone veneer. Profits sink when too many choices are available, which provides the opportunity for too many things to go wrong, and when buyers demand fulfillment of expensive warranty obligations. Pay attention to your builder's track record for coming back and fixing things under warranty.

TOP 10 BIG BUILDERS, 2011

Rank	Builder	Revenues	Closings
1	Pulte Group	$3,950,743,000	15,275
2	D.R. Horton	$3,665,523,000	17,176
3	Lennar Corporation	$2,624,785,000	10,845
4	NVR	$2,611,195,000	8,487
5	Toll Brothers	$1,475,882,000	2,611
6	KB Home	$1,305,299,000	5,812
7	Hovnanian Enterprises	$1,244,817,000	4,216
8	Standard Pacific Corporation	$895,943,773	2,563
9	The Ryland Group	$890,733,000	3,413
10	Meritage Homes Corporation	$860,884,000	3,268

Total Revenues: $19,525,804,773

Total Closings: 73,666

SOURCE: PROFESSIONAL BUILDER

LOCAL BUILDERS AND CONTRACTORS

Beyond the big corporations, a vast range of smaller companies provide houses. The smaller the firm, the more regional or local its coverage. Some middle-size firms may generate their own designs or else purchase licenses to build designs made by others. Local builders and general contractors, on the other hand, usually purchase the designs for their projects. They construct the smallest number of homes, and their services vary by the region where they operate, their resources, and their expertise.

Some builders construct **"spec" homes** ("spec" is short for "speculation") in the hope of attracting a buyer. Whether built in subdivisions or on random lots, spec homes pop up when builders need extra profit to put into their own ventures. Without a particular client to satisfy, builders can use whatever construction techniques and materials they want. Sometimes spec homes are completed only as far as erecting walls, adding roofs, and installing windows. The potential purchaser then gets to choose all the finishes and final details, which adds to the base price. Sometimes builders construct spec homes in a new development to augment the presence of a model home and to keep the new site from looking too bare. It is good to know about spec homes, but most buyers are more interested in the standard models that the building industry produces.

PLAN FACTORIES

Regardless of a building company's size, it must rely on architectural drawings in order to produce its houses. These drawings provide the basic stock of designs from which buyers make their purchases. While the biggest companies may generate plans from their in-house designers, many designs used by smaller home builders come from independent companies known as **plan factories.** In general, the smaller the builder, the more likely it is to use plans designed by others. Although no hard figures are available, it seems likely that most of the designs used in mass-produced housing have their origins in plan factories. Here is how it works in principle: a plan provider may sell a set of plans with a license to build a single house at a one-time cost of $1,300. Once licensed, plans that are often repeated can then net the designer $300 to $400 for each rebuild (Fig. 9). Some plan factories seek specific niches— one might offer Colonial designs, and another "Palladian"—and others offer a full

BRIEF HISTORY

JOSEPH EICHLER

Joseph Eichler (1900–1974) was a twentieth-century postwar American real estate developer who helped revolutionize the suburban tract home from the 1950s to the 1970s. Eichler, who was not an architect but, rather, acted as the builder and developer for his properties, hired several architects to execute specific plans that related to his residential design philosophy. Between 1949 and 1974, Eichler's company, Eichler Homes, constructed about 11,000 houses in California. Eichler was heavily influenced by the American architect Frank Lloyd Wright's Usonian home model, which focused on creating typically small, single-story dwellings for the middle-income American family, using native materials, natural lighting, and modernist architectural touches like flat roofs and simple geometric shapes. Eichler created a new and updated take on these principles, developing the "Eichler House," an offshoot that became more commonly known as "ranch-style housing." The term was used to describe the fresh, modernist approach of his tract houses.

spectrum. Once the plans are obtained, small builders sometimes patch together pieces and parts of different plans and then offer them as options. Redrawing the plans by another design firm probably breaches the license agreement, but it occasionally happens.

Traditionally, plan factories were a wholesale service provided directly to the building trade and were not available directly to (retail) buyers. But an increasing number of enterprises, of varying degrees of quality and reliability, are making plans available for purchase over the Internet. The **Stephen Fuller Designs** website provides an example of a company offering a wide variety of styles (Fig. 10). You can peruse its collection of preexisting house plans for designs for primary or secondary residences. Among the sixteen primary residence choices offered, you can click on the Country Heritage type and find a series of plans that fall under this category. Under the Woodbury Grove option, we find floor plans with room dimensions and elevations of the house. Square footage totals are included. If this is the design you want, you can then order drawings for construction, which you would present to a builder for building. Builders might even buy these plans for their own use. The

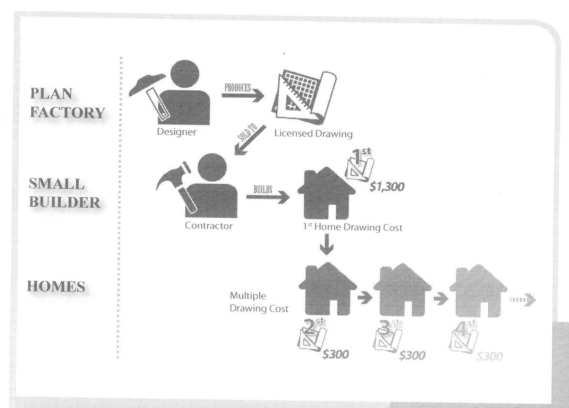

Fig. 9: The relationship between plan factory and small builders.

STEPHEN FULLER
D E S I G N S

WELCOME TO THE NEW StephenFuller.com – AMERICA'S HOME FOR CLASSIC DESIGN

CUSTOM HOMES

WE HAVE LEARNED over the past twenty-five years of practice that "places" are not easily defined – the architecture of today is not about designing *places*; it's about designing a *sense of place*. We must respond to modern lifestyles while respecting and celebrating all that is great about the past.

WE HAVE A PASSION for turning dreams and ideas into physical expressions of our love of classic design. From the first line we draw until the last brick is laid, our unfaltering devotion to our craft results in beautifully inspiring places, grounded by precedent, but always of our time.

WE ARE STEPHEN FULLER DESIGNS. We design houses, communities, gathering places, and more. All are places to be inspired by... all are places to call "home".

Featured on Houzz

—— CHOOSE FROM THE OPTIONS BELOW TO VIEW SELECTIONS OF OUR WORK ——

CUSTOM HOMES

RENOVATIONS

NEIGHBORHOODS

COMMERCIAL

HOUSE PLANS

CLASSIC PLACES BLOG

Become a Member | Member Login | Contact Us | Privacy Statement | Terms & Conditions | Return / Refund Policy | About Us

Stephen Fuller, Inc.
House Plans, Floor Plans, Blue Prints and Construction Documents created by Stephen Fuller, have all right, title, and interest reserved by Stephen Fuller ®, Inc © 2012 Stephen Fuller®, Inc.

Fig. 10: Stephen Fuller Designs, home page.

fees charged depend on the number of construction sets ordered as well as any options you might select, such as an 18" x 24" rendering of the house. What you are purchasing is, in effect, a license to construct a house according to a preexisting design. You can buy and build the same design as anyone else can throughout the country. In Part III, we will look in more detail at the pros and cons of purchasing your building plans online.

DEVELOPERS

Who runs this show, and how do subdivisions get built in their specific locations? There is no single, simple answer to these questions, but generally developers, either as builders or entrepreneurs, control the process. Although you might think that cities, towns, and municipalities or regional authorities determine where communities get built, developers have great influence on the decision-making process, and those decisions affect transportation, environmental health, and overall vitality in a region. Cities do make long-term plans, but they may be ignored or made useless by waivers, incentives, and special deals. Competing interests are at work in the U.S. housing system, and the economic power and political clout of developers are usually behind the ultimate decisions about what gets built, where, and when. New highways are laid out on city peripheries, where land is cheap; old highways are widened to facilitate development. Off these highways are the future building sites for single-family homes and shopping centers. Underlying this kind of development are the following assumptions: populations will continue to grow; people will continue to rely on automobiles; and, regardless of economic recessions and unemployment, people will be able to buy new homes.

Some developers plan and build their own housing communities. Others buy land, divide it into lots, develop infrastructure (roads and utilities), and then sell the lots to builders. The builders either build spec houses for future sales or sign on buyers and build a "custom" house for them. Some developers use a combination of both approaches: building spec homes and selling lots to other builders. And some building companies may take control of the entire process, even offering financing for the purchase of homes.

Just as there is no single client type, there is no single developer profile. They range from individuals working locally to corporations operating nationally or internationally. Many developers establish special niches, for example, commercial office buildings or specialty building types like health care centers; our focus is on the developer of single-family residential housing.

How does a person become a developer? No professional training is required nor do regulating or licensing agencies control their practices as in law, medicine, accounting, architecture, and other fields. In the housing field, a developer is someone with access to capital who creates deals involving land purchase and sales. He or she often provides infrastructure for their projects and markets the properties as well. The existence of developers is a testament to the American dream that almost anyone with ambition, energy, drive, and, sometimes, luck can assemble the funds to produce a dream for others. Putting aside the unfortunate forays of developers into unproductive or disastrous ventures, we owe to them the creation of the bulk of American suburbs.

With access to capital and an awareness of the economic impact that a development can have on a community, developers have political power, and in another great American tradition, they use that power to further their business interests. At times their interests conflict with the well-being of a community. Such clashes will increase as stresses on natural resources like land and water intensify, and will increase the cost of public amenities like transportation, open space, and utilities, including sewage and water treatment.

The opportunities for a small-scale self-made developer can be seen in the small Monticello development just outside the city limits of Austin, Texas (Fig. 11). A local individual purchased half the side of a big hill called Mt. Larson from a developer who had bought it from the original landowner. The land never had been built upon because its steep, sloping terrain made construction impractical. Furthermore, several of the views, though picturesque, face the unrelenting western sun, which can be broiling hot during a Central Texas summer. Most of the lots were sold to local builders, who either erected spec houses or marketed the lots for sale to prospective buyers. Perhaps the most interesting aspect of this development was the differences between Thomas Jefferson's Monticello, the gated community's namesake, and the houses built there, all of which come from previously existing design types that are more "modern Tuscan" in theme than the neoclassical designs favored by the American president.

BRIEF HISTORY

LEVITTOWN

Levittown is America's archetypal suburban development, built by the influential and important building firm of Levitt & Sons. Between 1947 and 1951, Abraham Levitt and his sons, William and Alfred, built over 17,000 houses on a former potato field in Long Island, New York. The early Levittown house was very affordable, and it fulfilled the home-ownership dreams of America soldiers returning after World War II. Levitt & Sons turned the entire subdivision into a house-building assembly line by using standardized labor and interchangeable parts. Instead of the houses moving down an assembly line, like cars in a manufacturing plant, teams of nonunion workers moved from site to site, performing specific tasks. Using this technique, the Levitts reportedly built thirty houses a day, at a rate of one house every sixteen minutes. Buyers could choose from a few basic house plans with a small number of variations. By the early 1960s, some critics had attacked Levittown houses for their similarity, but they had provided, at least temporarily, a dream home for generations of first-time home buyers in a housing boom that forever changed the feel of the American suburb.

Below: Levittown, Pennsylvania, ca. 1959.

FURTHER INFORMATION

"INFILL HOUSES"

Some developers specialize in adding new houses to existing neighborhoods by filling in empty lots or tearing down existing building stock and replacing it with new houses. An example of infill can be seen in Washington, D.C., in an area just west of American University in the neighborhood encompassing Chain Bridge Road and University Terrace. Traditionally, the area had comfortable single-family houses on very large wooded lots. The houses varied in size and style, and the area attracted well-off buyers. As land values in this desirable neighborhood rose, developers were motivated to build on lots previously considered unusable or to tear down older homes and replace a single structure with several new houses. These processes are affecting many neighborhoods elsewhere. A local resident turned developer constructed eight new houses in the neighborhood, including his own residence. A graduate of Georgetown University with a degree in political science, he is self-taught when it comes to developing. He represents an exceptional approach in catering to high-end demand, and his range is geographically limited.

Fig. 11: Development signage.

MEDIA

Finally, we look at the media as a player in the housing process. We have already noted that magazines and newspapers provided a central means of disseminating images of American homes, and of shopping for them, for much of the twentieth century, and they still are informative. Some buyers may buy their plans from magazines, even though they could afford to hire an architect to design a unique house for them.

One reason that buyers prefer quickly available plans is the ubiquity of images we see on television, at the movies, and on the Internet. One source of domestic images comes from sitcoms on television. Images remain vivid for many baby boomers of the sitcom homes of the Cleaver family in *Leave it to Beaver,* the Ricardos in *I Love Lucy,* and the Bradys of *The Brady Bunch,* whose family father was an architect, though rarely at work. Their style, décor, spaces, and implied floor plans, as

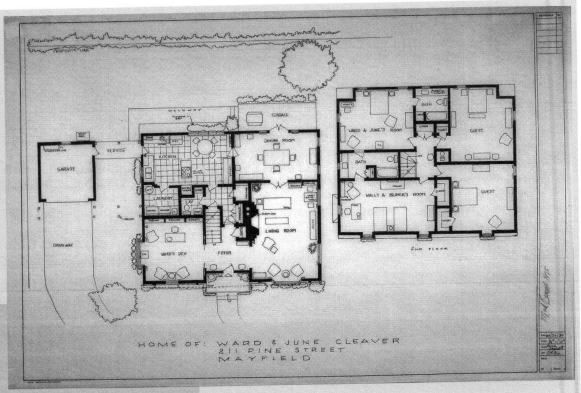

Fig. 12: Home of the Cleaver Family, courtesy of Mark Bennet.

recalled by the artist Mark Bennett, worked their way into our consciousness, subtly affected what was considered comfortable and what we aspired to (Fig. 12).

Images of the grand American house emerged in the depiction of Southfork Ranch on the TV series *Dallas*. The series began on April 2, 1978, and ran in over 130 countries for 356 episodes over thirteen years and in reruns around the world (Fig. 13). It not only presented a house in an updated setting of the American west, but also communicated a particular lifestyle and set of values. The series was so popular that an updated version was prepared for TV in 2012. The repercussions of such widespread images are vast. From the ranch of the Ewing family to the smaller interior spaces of Lucy and Ricky's New York apartment, specific images of home entered the minds of millions of people. Relatively recently, cable television has greatly expanded people's range of images and experiences regarding every aspect of domestic life. One of the most effective cable sources is HGTV. Launched in 1994 and initially conceived as the Home, Lawn and Garden Channel, it provides approximately sixty programs to its widespread audience. The themes of these programs have been consistently about home building, remodeling, gardening,

Fig. 13: Ultimate Texas ranch.

landscaping, decorating, and design as well as crafts and hobbies. Reaching 94 million households via cable in the United States, Canada, Japan, and other countries, its impact on our taste in housing and our knowledge about the home is almost too vast to grasp. It is no wonder then that we find McMansions in Ireland and new Tuscan villas in China. Digital media unites us all in the quest for our dream home.

We have looked at players involved in the housing industry overall and now will take a journey that is the first step in the process of buying your new home.

KNOW THE PLAYERS, KNOW THE MARKET

- **The Buyers** -- you the consumer

- **The Marketers** -- people who are trying to sell you a house

- **Big Builders** -- major players in housing industry

- **Local Builders** -- regional builders providing local home construction services; some construct "spec" homes

- **Plan Factories** -- companies that produce and supply architectural drawings for house construction to builders, sometimes directly to future home owners

- **Developers** -- builders or entrepreneurs with great influence on the decision-making of land use and community building

- **Media** -- TV shows and programs that communicate a particular lifestyle and set of values to viewers

Notes

PART II

The Visit

PREPARATIONS

An event as major as buying a home requires study and advanced preparation. At a minimum, look at the real estate section of your local newspapers, consider sources online, get recommendations from friends, and look at magazines to see what kinds of houses you like and don't like. Also, take the time to write down a list of your own requirements for a new house and take a realistic look at your budget.

As previously mentioned, the real estate sections of newspapers can inform you about the available building stock in a town or region and about plans for any future housing developments. Ads often provide specific details about location, price, and, often briefly, pictures of housing stock.

Magazines have provided images of homes for over a century. So-called **shelter magazines** vary in quality and focus. Some include floor plans and building designs, and others concentrate on interiors like kitchens and living rooms. They allow potential home buyers to discover the latest stylistic trends. Generations of buyers have cut pictures out of magazine and assembled scrapbooks that are diaries of aspirations and dreams.

Numerous books cater to homebuyers. Some feature grand homes in a variety of styles, mostly with pictures and minimal text. Many of these books are subsidized by the architects whose work appears within. They often appeal to the luxury market and to those with an interest in unique homes. Other books focus on small houses that are more efficient and less costly, the idea being that smaller is better. The **small-house phenomenon** has created a successful cottage industry with an interested readership and has had the positive effect of asking questions about our lifestyles: do we need all that space found in big houses? The basic assumption of the small-house movement is that if an informed client hires a receptive architect, the client can get a design that is both efficient and attractive. This approach has appeal for the one-of-a-kind house, but it is limited: it may be more expensive per square foot than a tract house and does not provide a large-scale economic model for mass housing.

As part of your preparations for deciding on a dream home, you may want to visit a Parade of Homes, a showcase for the most recent work of local builders. **Parades of Homes** are found throughout the country. Advertised well in advance, they give the public and potential buyers a chance to see the work of several builders at one time. Builders construct model homes as a means of introducing you to their work. They collaborate with their suppliers, who likewise see the event as a chance to demonstrate their products and introduce their services to potential clients. Each model is filled with modern amenities and furniture, making it feel like a department store showroom. Usually, the homes available for inspection are fully landscaped too. The Parade of Homes is a marketing tool, particularly effective at the local and regional level, and especially for smaller and medium sized builders who are competing one on one with houses next to or near each other.

The event provides a sampler, resembling a smorgasbord with each entry competing to be your favorite dish. In going from one house to the next, you compare the differences between builders' approaches—and the similarities. You can meet builders, contractors, and designers and pick up brochures and pamphlets that describe their services. Of course, the builder you ultimately choose may not be participating in the Parade of Homes, but having visited one, your own knowledge has increased.

With some general ideas about the kind of design that appeals to you, and perhaps having seen attractive home models at a Parade of Homes, you need to think seriously about the key influences on your dream home: location, access, communities and neighborhoods, home owners associations, and layouts and lots.

Location: It's the first consideration. Most building sites are situated on the edges of cities or even beyond the edges. The land there is least expensive for the

BRIEF HISTORY

SHELTER MAGAZINES

The popular home, or "shelter," magazines date back to the turn of the twentieth century. The earliest examples included House Beautiful (1896), The Craftsman (1901), House and Garden (1901), and Better Homes & Gardens (1922). Women's magazines geared toward homemakers predated shelter magazines. The Ladies' Home Journal (1883), originally oriented to housewives, was one of the first popular magazines to regularly publish home plans. Shelter magazines proliferated in the 1950s, when they became instrumental to the home-building industry as outlets for ideas on stylistic trends and taste. In many instances, architects pay the magazines to have their work published, so some glossy magazines are little more than extended advertisements.

Left: *House Beautiful,* March 1969.
Right: *Better Homes & Gardens,* September 1930.

Left: *House & Garden,* January-June 1922.
Right: *The Craftsman,* October 1901.

FURTHER INFORMATION

PARADE OF HOMES

In 1948, following World War II, the NAHB began organizing annual Parade of Homes events as a way to publicize the progress of the house-building industry specific to their regional building associations: new construction techniques, building materials, and domestic designs and styles. Historically, the events featured publicity stunts like beauty contests, games, street parties, and public speeches by celebrities and politicians, including American presidents. These Parades are presently still very much a part of the American housing industry culture and occur annually in hundreds of cities, attracting thousands of visitors who hope to see the newest in home building. If you visit one of your city's Parade of Homes, you will be able to walk through a series of new model houses representing the latest products available from your local builders. Each model will be staged with modern amenities and furniture, making it feel like a department store showroom.

developer and builder, and may have special features such as hills, views, or trees. The cost of land is fundamental to the price of your home. Basic infrastructure—roads, utilities, water, and sewage systems—figure into the cost. At the low-priced end of market, land cost is particularly critical. The cheapest land is often found on flat sites with minimal or no natural features in locations far out of town. One factor to consider in visiting any subdivision is the possibility that early buyers may get a discount on price or free options as a way to get the project rolling. When a subdivision is almost complete and few houses are available, prices may be higher.

Fundamental in considering locations are **property taxes** and **school systems.** For families with children, the quality of neighborhood schools will be important. And property taxes are a major ongoing, and increasing, expense. Always find out about the expenses and use them in comparing one location with another.

Access: Getting to and from your new home raises the question of transportation. Generally, the unspoken assumption about housing developments is that you drive to, from, and within a subdivision in your own car. The farther away you live from work and other daily objectives, the more you will pay in gas and transportation costs. Certainly, some commuters share vans, and in some instances public transportation is available. But generally builders don't consider how you will get to or from the site (other than locating a subdivision near at least one major highway or freeway). In an age of soaring gas prices, worsening traffic, and ensuing air pollution, the location of subdivisions may become a consideration for builders and the governmental entities that grant them development rights. You need to ask yourself: what is the relationship between the location of your home and the places where you work and shop?

Communities and neighborhoods: When you buy a house in a subdivision, you are not only buying a home but also becoming part of a neighborhood. Increasingly, the term "neighborhood" is being replaced by the idea of community. Big builders show clients entire "communities" with models of the best-selling houses. The sense of buying into a community as well as a house is a significant factor in the whole system of housing production.

Communities have specific packages of amenities attached to them. The packages, which may include schools, sport facilities, shopping areas, and green spaces, are adjusted for the target audience. In principle, neighborhood amenities vary depending on the demographics of the residents; for example, different groups of amenities will be offered for communities composed primarily of aging baby boomers, singles with no children, or people married with children. The specifics of a neighborhood package are worked out in detail, and they add to the value of the houses themselves. For many buyers, it's not just stores and sports facilities that are appealing, but also organized activities, concerts, wine clubs, and other affinity groups, all of which are coordinated by social media, including Facebook and dedicated web pages. For people new to an area, the sense that you immediately can fit into a community of individuals from similar economic and social backgrounds may be more important than what your house looks like.

Home Owners Associations: Closely associated with the planning of communities in subdivisions is a home owners association, or HOA. Looking into the operation of the local HOA before buying a home should be a priority for you. An HOA enforces rules about what is allowed to be built or changed, and what isn't. Sometimes HOAs are professionally managed and paid for by fees that all home owners pay, and sometimes they consist of a board of home owners. The HOA may have authority to decide what are acceptable additions or changes to your home, such as the materials used for your façade or even your roof. It may determine where children are allowed to play, as well as a host of other rules. The intention of the HOA is to maintain the value of all property in the community, to ensure uniformity, and to guarantee a good level of minimal maintenance and upkeep.

Layouts and lots: Neighborhoods and house sites are planned as part of the design of the subdivision itself. This is design at the largest scale, in which the land is divided up into parcels with dimensions assigned to each lot, roads are drawn in, and future utilities noted. Regardless of whether the layout is done in-house in a big building firm or subcontracted to a freelancer, the layout requires the skills of a civil engineer, surveyor, or similar professional. The overriding goal in laying out a subdivision is to design lots that provide, when sold, maximum profit for the developer. It seems obvious that more lots mean bigger profits, and in fact, putting as many lots as possible in a development has been the guiding practice. But developers now realize that setting aside some space as greenbelts or parks instead of house lots has marketing advantages and adds value to the subdivision as a whole. Furthermore, some governmental entities that authorize developments may require them to include green spaces, flood-control features, or areas for the recharge of groundwater from rains and snow, and such restrictions affect the number of lots allowed in a subdivision.

Even when open spaces are figured into a subdivision layout, the configuration of streets and lots generally shows very little difference from site designs made a century ago. Large feeder roads connect smaller roads ending in cul-de-sacs (a street that terminates with a circular turnaround resembling a sack). Lots are rectangular, with their short ends fronting the street. These lots are drawn up using simple geometric forms incorporating the minimum dimensions necessary for the construction of a single house. The effects of climate, particularly sun, wind, and temperature, on a house are not considered, and the lots are assumed to be flat. As we will see later in looking at the pluses and minus of tract homes, those two points—**orientation and site topography**—are significant factors in determining whether your new home is a dream or a nightmare.

RECAP

THINGS TO CONSIDER
When Planning Your Dream Home

- ☐ **Location**
  - ☐ School District
    - ☐ Elementary
    - ☐ Middle
    - ☐ High school
- ☐ **Property Taxes**
- ☐ **Transportation and Access**
  - ☐ Proximity to major thoroughfares and streets
  - ☐ Proximity to work, school, shopping and other daily activities
  - ☐ Proximity to public transportation
- ☐ **Communities and Neighborhoods**
  - ☐ Parks and Recreation
  - ☐ Community Centers
  - ☐ Multi-use Complex or Space
- ☐ **Home Owners Associations (HOAs)**
- ☐ **Orientation and Site Topography**
  - ☐ Sun Orientation
  - ☐ Slope or Flat Site
  - ☐ Existing Vegetation on Site
  - ☐ Nearby Building Heights

- ☐ **Layout and Lots**
  - ☐ Lot Square Footage _____
  - ☐ Home Square Footage _____
  - ☐ Lot Style (rectangular, irregular, sloped)
  - ☐ Landscaping _____
  - ☐ Number of Bedrooms _____
  - ☐ Number of Baths _____
  - ☐ Kitchen
    - ☐ Style
    - ☐ Kitchen Island
    - ☐ Bar Seating
    - ☐ Type of Countertop
    - ☐ Type of Cabinet
- ☐ **Dining Room**
- ☐ **Family Room**
- ☐ **Living Room**
- ☐ **Additional Rooms**
- ☐ **Additional Amenities**
- ☐ **Selecting Your Builder**
  - ☐ Name of Company _____
  - ☐ Plan Model _____

- ☐ **Budget, Price Range**

  _____

CASE STUDY 1: FAIRWAY ESTATES

You've begun preparing yourself to shop for a house. Let's take what you've learned on a visit to two typical sites operated by two different kinds of developers. Our first visit is to the neighborhood containing Fairway Estates, a gated subdivision at Circle C Ranch in Austin, Texas, a master-planned community that could stand for any of hundreds of similar sites around the country. This subdivision, built by **KB Home,** a major national builder focused on select regions of the United States, features medium- to higher-priced homes. In early 2013, the prices of homes in Fairway Estates were around the high end of its local offerings, just under $570,000 for a two-story, four-to-five-bedroom, 4,800-square-foot house with a three-car garage. As the name implies, many of the lots lie along a golf course. KB has two other subdivisions nearby, one priced at midlevel and the other at the low end of the price range. A basic home in subdivisions located farther out of town can cost as little as $166,000. Because prices can change rapidly, and are even subject to special sales, I recommend that you check current prices, like those at KB Home, on builders' websites. Regardless of size, amenities, or price, the process of visiting, inspecting, and buying a home is much the same.

There is one particular difference at Fairway Estates: many of the homebuyers there are hoping to **trade up** from houses that they already own in the development. This implies they are pleased with what they already know and familiar with, and clearly like living in the neighborhood. Some buyers are trading up to larger homes, others are opting for smaller residences—choices that mirror personal economic conditions, family status, and just the desire for change. Until recently, Americans' choices in housing have reflected mobility—people typically lived in their mass-production homes for about seven years before moving.

Fairway Estates is located at the southwest end of Austin and on the west side of Circle C Ranch, a development established over the last twenty-five years (Fig. 14). KB Home bought the land for Fairway Estates and two adjoining developments in 2003 when an earlier developer went bankrupt. Because the development had a history, a number of neighborhood amenities were already in place.

We are going to visit a model home to see for ourselves what the houses in Fairway Estates look like. En route, we notice the neighborhood includes the Escarpment Village Shopping Center, a swim center, a park, an elementary school, a site designated for a second swim center, and along one side of Fairway Estates, a

 Neighborhood Layout

Circle C Ranch

N

🏠 Model Park
🏠 Circle C - Enclave Estates
🏠 Circle C - The Enclave
🏠 Circle C - Fairway Estates
🏠 Open Space and Drainage

Swim Center

Park

Escarpment Village Shopping Center

ESCARPMENT

Elementary School

Swim Center Coming Soon

Golf Course

5/10

 © 2010 KB Home (KBH). This map is for general orientation purposes and is not drawn to scale. KB Home does not represent or guarantee the map to be accurate and it remains subject to change or modification at any time without notice. KB Home does not control, and neither KB Home nor any of its sales counselors or representatives makes any representations or guarantees regarding future development of the community or uses adjacent to or in proximity to the community. This map does not constitute any representation or guarantee that the community or surrounding area will be built out, developed or operated as shown.

Fig. 14: Neighborhood plan, Fairway Estates, KB Home, Austin, Texas.

Fig. 15: Model home, Fairway Estates.

private golf course. A supermarket is nearby. The presence or absence of amenities is a key point in considering where you want to live. Here, schools and a swim center will appeal to families with children but not necessarily to singles or empty nesters without children.

We time our trip after the morning commute and before the afternoon return, so for the moment we can ignore traffic issues. In these between times, the wide streets, some of which have planted medians, make for easy and comfortable access. Because a model home is open for visitors, the gates to Fairway Estates are left open. The impact of a model home is important for a builder: people tend to select for their home the exact model that they visit, even when they can choose from ten other variations in floor plans and elevations. This tendency points to an important indicator: people find comfort in fewer choices rather than an overwhelming number of options. It also shows how difficult it is to imagine a physical space from two-dimensional drawings. Exploring an actual built house, particularly observing all its furnishings, gives people a real and concrete feel for what they might or might not want in their own home. Encountering the physical reality of a model home is a major factor in shaping what choices you will make when you pick the details to define your own residence, including the floor plan, elevations, material selections, and other furnishings.

Today, we are visiting the model home called the **Augusta.** Christy, who works for KB Home, has opened the home for us and will explain and introduce the house; she has worked for the builder for about ten months but has several years of experience working either as a real estate agent or for other builders. The Augusta is one of twelve models in Fairway Estates. It comprises 4,811 square feet on two floors; that size alone tells us we are at the high end of the product spectrum (Fig. 15). The furnishings, layout, colors, and accessories that we will see are the result of having a specialist "stage," or design, the interior of the model home. Normally, these interior designers work exclusively for building companies and do not provide services to the general public. The staged ambience has a big impact on your perception of the value of the home. The best materials, appliances and furnishings are selected, but they are not included in the **base price** of the house, which covers only standard options. The price for this model starts at $543,995; so we could say it is in the high end of builder homes, but not in the ultra-luxury category. Not surprised, we see that size and price are interconnected.

The first feature we notice is the landscaped yard; it has trees, bushes, and grass nicely laid out. This **landscaping,** which can give the impression of lush green and a natural setting, has a greater impact on us than we might expect. Knowing its ability to give a warm impression, builders generally don't hesitate to invest in landscaping the fronts of model homes, even lower-priced ones. The cost of the lot's landscaping is, however, not included in the base price for your home; it is an add-on. Our lot size is the same size as all the other lots in Fairway Estates: 100 feet wide by 150 feet in length, a typical size for an upscale development. Lots along the adjoining golf course are larger. If there are no trees that might affect the placement of the house, the average front **setback** from the street is about 35 feet. The setbacks on the sides of the houses to the property line are 5 feet; side setbacks are always an important dimension, since they determine how close you are to you neighbor. Here you will live 10 feet from your neighbors on either side. In addition to the landscaping, we also notice immediately the front **façade** of the model home. "Façade" refers to the "face" of a building, and at KB Home the front façade is available in three styles. But we are eager to see how the interior works, so we will return to look a bit closer at the façades after touring the interior.

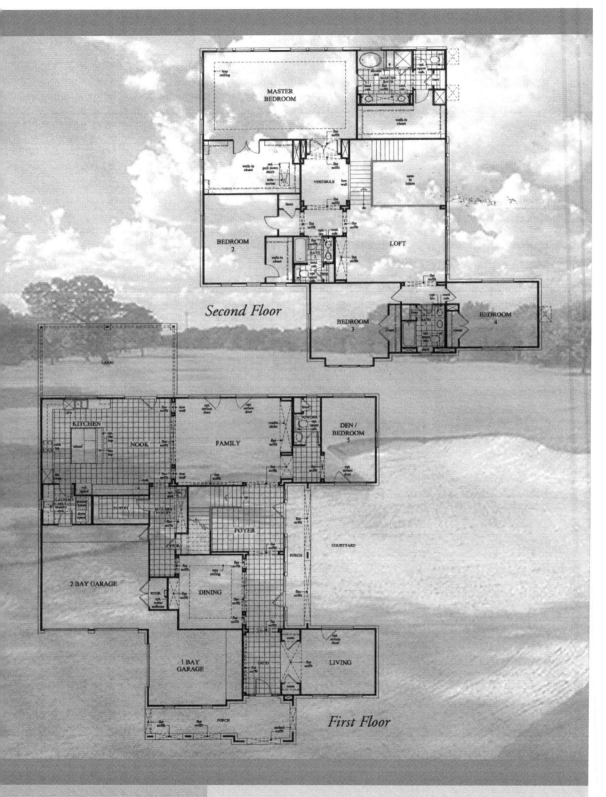

Second Floor

First Floor

Fig. 16: Plan, Augusta model home.

I'll describe our tour of the house in some detail to help you be more aware of the spaces you'll encounter on the tours you take. Most people enter their homes from their garages, but our model home has a temporary sales office in its garage, so we will enter through the front door (Figs. 16, 17). Upon entering, we see on our right a formal living room; this recalls the old tradition of having a parlor at the front of the house, facing the street. Set apart from much of the other living spaces, people now tend to use this room less. As we saw earlier, surveys show that only buyers of very high-end houses prefer to have one. People just don't want formal living rooms as they once did, and they have started to be phased out in the design of some new tract homes. As we move straight through the foyer, we see on the left a dining room and on the right a door that leads to a narrow long porch looking out on our side yard. Beyond the dining room, the foyer opens up to the stairs leading to the second floor. Straight ahead on the ground level is the family room. When we first enter the family room from the foyer, we see on the right a powder room and a multiuse space that could be either a "den" or more likely an office or ground-floor bedroom. The space of the family room itself connects without any separation to a nook and the open kitchen. Combined, this is the largest space in the entire house, which tells us that much of the life within will occur in this area. A door opens off the kitchen to the outside in a space KB Home calls a **lanai.** The word comes from the Hawaiian language; the space is basically a back porch.

At the end of the counter next to the refrigerator is the entry to a **butler's pantry.** Your chances of having a butler are remote, but this is a space designed to store household items. A door from the pantry leads into a second storage room. On the opposite side of the kitchen is the laundry room, which leads to a two-bay garage. From the two-bay garage, we can move into a one-bay garage, which can be used for a third vehicle or, as is often the case, for storage of additional items like lawnmowers, bicycles, and out-of-season sports equipment.

Returning to the interior through the laundry room past the kitchen and into the family room, we now proceed on our tour up the stairs to the second floor (Fig. 18). It ends in a loft-like space open to the stairwell and the first floor. How this space is used is not immediately obvious; children could use it as a play area, or it could be a media center. Whatever noise occurs in it can be heard downstairs. Beyond the loft are two bedrooms, for children or guests. The other side has a storage space and leads to a third bedroom, which includes a walk-in closet and an adjacent bathroom. We pass a square vestibule with a low wall on the right side looking over the stairwell, and we enter into the master bedroom suite. It includes two walk-in closets, one larger than the other, and a bathroom with an oval tub, shower, and two separate sinks. The master bedroom has windows on two sides. It also has an elaborated ceiling designed to make the room feel special: the ceiling is flattened at the edges to create the impression of a "tray."

The usual route into a house through a garage goes through a utility room, which often has laundry facilities and no natural light (Fig. 19). From there we enter the kitchen and onward to the other spaces of the house. As you can see, the

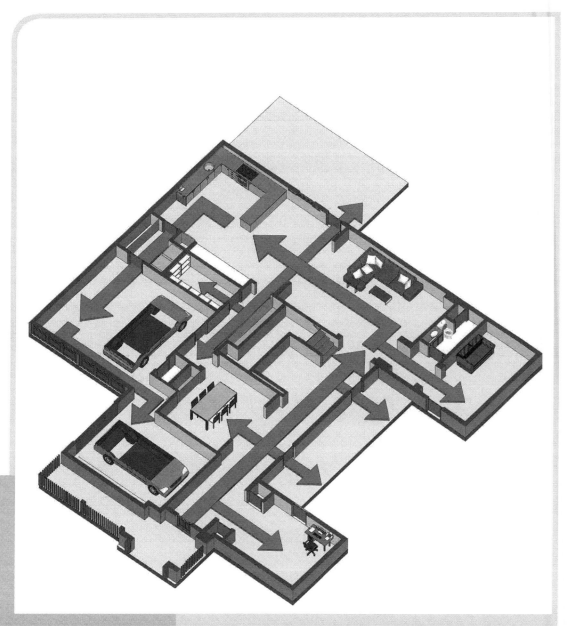

Fig. 17: Entry sequence to Augusta model home from front door.

experience from garage to kitchen is very different from the trip through the front door to the great space; the former is more utilitarian, the latter more formal or almost ceremonial.

To summarize our tour of the interior, we've seen a living room (little used), a dining area, an open kitchen with eating nook, a central family room, a laundry room, storage areas, and a pantry. There are 3.5 baths, some large closets, and four bedrooms, including a master suite. The garage space holds up to three vehicles. The

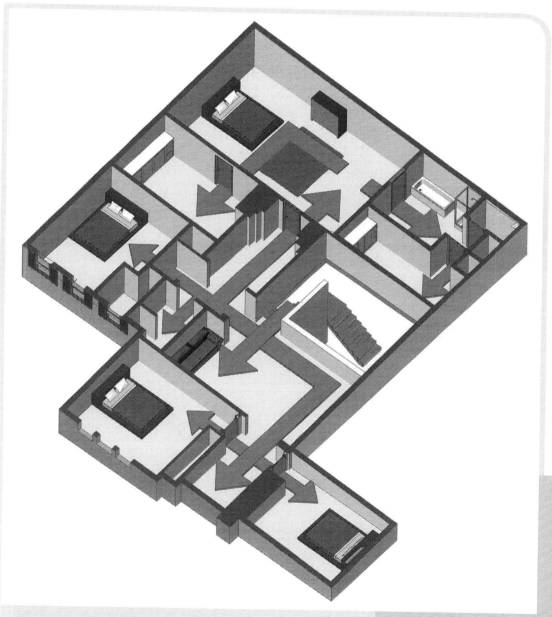

Fig. 18: Second floor, Augusta model home.

ceiling heights of about ten feet are impressive, a factor that adds to the feeling of openness in the house. In lower-priced tract homes, the ceiling height is significantly lower, which changes our experience of the spaces.

The arrangement of spaces is recorded in a drawing called a **floor plan.** The floor plan for the Augusta is shown in Fig. 16. It is a two-dimensional graphic device that both describes the house design and serves as the basis for construction. If you are not familiar with floor plans, or if they seem incomprehensible, you can learn to "read" floor plans with a little practice. If you have any questions, ask your salesperson or real estate agent to walk you through the floor plans of a model home or any other home that interests you. Each floor of a house should have its own plan.

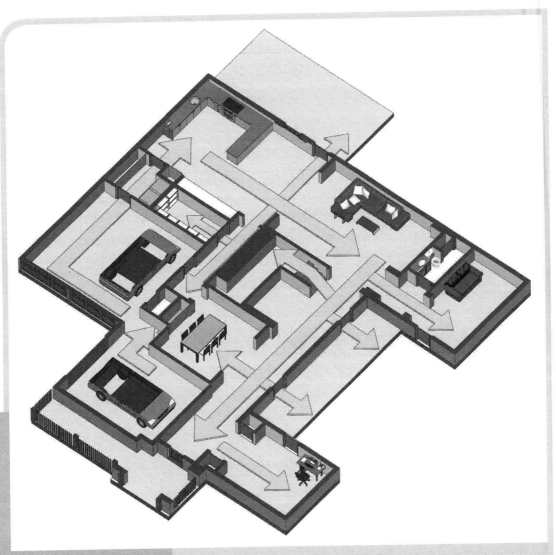

Fig. 19: Entry sequence to Augusta model home from garage.

FAÇADES

Having toured the interior, we next go outside to look at the exterior **façade.** Discussions about the impact of façades are almost nonexistent in the housing business, and as a result people know very little about their significance on the image of their homes.

A façade can either directly relate to the interior or be independent of the interior. When a façade expresses what happens on the interior, we tend to assume that the form and function of the house are connected. For instance, a change of materials or the special placement of windows on the exterior can mark the location of an interior staircase. When the façade and interiors don't correspond, they are said to be independent and unconnected. Looking from the outside at an independent two-story façade, you have no indication where the staircase might be. In the twentieth century, many progressive architects believed that a façade correlating the interior and exterior was more "honest" or "true" than a façade that gave no indication of the activities within.

Most people who buy builder houses are unconcerned with the "truth" of façades. They do respond, however, to subtle visual cues that façades communicate.

DEFINITION

The word **"façade,"** from French, suggests the face of a building. Just as our own faces tell us much about our characters and identities, a façade communicates something about the meaning and identity of a home. Like a human face, however, the façade may be subtler or more complicated than we assume. People may appear unaware of the façade of a house, but its design and structure still speak to us, our neighbors, and the world at large.

The façades of homes are drawn as **elevations.** While the floor plan shows the horizontal plane, elevations are graphic representations of vertical surfaces of a building; they show interior or exterior views of the whole side of a building or the walls of a room. They tend to look flat when seen as two-dimensional pictures, but if drawn with colors to indicate materials and with shading or shadows, they may appear livelier. A **perspective** view is an image that shows the façades of a building, but seems to put them into three-dimensional space. Perspective views tend to make the house appear more recognizably real.

Fig. 20: Classic elevation, Augusta model home.

Traditionally, the styles of houses, as expressed on façades, were even more revealing about what a home says about its identity and, by extension, about your identity in buying one.

At Fairway Estates, each of the twelve models is available in three styles, based on the front elevation of the house: Classic, Texas Traditional, and Country French. Let's look at these three styles, but remember that the floor plans for these styles are fixed; the elevation is like a jacket or outer garment that fits over the same shirt and pants.

In the **Classic** elevation of the Augusta, the steep pitched roof has two dormers at the attic level (Fig. 20), a projection of the bedroom on the second level, and a roof gable with a small round vent. The entry has a pitched roof and an arched entry. The formal living room has two windows set in arches with dark keystones at their centers. Although we usually think of round or fluted columns when we think of classical architecture (such as Greek or Roman buildings and the imitations of them), in this elevation the arches, keystones, round vent, and brick veneer are intended to convey the idea of "classic."

The **Texas Traditional** elevation is applied to the same house by changing the detailing and materials, from brick to limestone (Fig. 21). Limestone is used for lintels—the beams over openings like the garages and windows. It differs from the

Fig. 21: Texas Traditional elevation, Augusta model home.

Classic version by having a protruding bay window and by changing the arrangement of the other windows.

In the **Country French** elevation, which is the façade of the model home we toured, the windows over the garage have different shutters from the other two styles, and the two attic windows have round tops instead of pitched coverings as in the Classic (Fig. 22). The window above the main entry is taller and narrow. At the ground level, the roof extends over the two windows to the left of the front door, suggesting a covered porch. The posts and corner brackets imply a rustic feeling. The most notable feature of the Country French elevation is the extension of the roof that swoops downward with a slight curve. The construction materials are rubble stone applied as a veneer, stucco, and composition shingles for the roof.

The differences in façade styles come from the substitution of materials and small details intended in a general way to communicate associations with the past or with a generalized place. The three styles have far more in common than they are different: roofs with the same pitch, bay windows, and **segmental arches** over some of the windows.

The Classic elevation is classic only in the sense that it might mean "the traditional standard." While there is no single classic elevation in Western

Fig. 22: Country French elevation, Augusta model home.

architecture—Greek and Roman styles varied widely—**classical elevations** usually were designed by using proportional systems, relating, for instance, height to width, and often had columns, bases, and single, unified roof treatments.

Likewise, the Texas Traditional elevation relies more on the **idea** of tradition than on true Texas vernacular architecture, the kinds of buildings that developed over time from necessities of use, climate, and available materials. (Vernacular architecture can be thought of as the architecture of the people rather than elite institutions.) The prototypes of Texas architecture can be seen particularly in rural settings in barns and outbuildings. In more urban locations, a version of Texas traditional in one town may be quite a bit different from that found in another, and both may be influenced by other currently popular styles. A traditional stone house of the later nineteenth century in Austin may vary dramatically from a house of the same period in San Antonio.

Similarly, with respect to the Country French elevation, there is no single style in France (or in the history of architecture) that is called "Country

DEFINITION

A **segmental arch** *has a portion of a half circle as its radius, not a complete half circle.*

French." The idea comes from people's **associations** with details and materials. Here, the arches, shutters, wood brackets, and swooping roof are intended to communicate something country and something French. At best, these associations can be only vague. While a deeply curving roof may recall an Alsatian vernacular architecture from eastern France, the same treatment also recalls English cottage architecture, even though the two have different vernacular roots.

This approach to designing façades applies broadly throughout the housing industry and can be found in most production housing throughout the United States. Who cares if the façade of a home and its interior have nothing to do with each other? What difference does it make?

To answer these questions, let's go back to clothes for a moment. Everyday jeans and a T-shirt convey casual, relaxed informality, usually without much coordination between top and bottom. A beautiful gown may have variation in its details as well as contrasting materials, but it becomes beautiful only when we sense its harmony or coherence. A blouse with pants and an accessory, each chosen with the others in mind, might convey elegance and simplicity. A sports coat, a fine cotton shirt, and tailored pants may communicate a similar image, though slightly more masculine in feel. When a suit is coordinated—with top, bottom, shoes, blouse, and jewelry in relation to one another—we have a clothing façade that connects form and function. When clothes are selected as independent items, like jeans and a tuxedo shirt, we have a **façade of mix-and-match.** Either look can be pleasing. The issue in fashion is less about formality versus informality than about uniformity versus variety. The same issue applies to architectural façades. In trying to understand either fashion or the image of the home, it helps to understand the difference between uniformity and mix-and-match.

THE OVERALL EXPERIENCE

Now that we have a picture of the interior layout and the façade, let's look more closely at the whole house, and our experience of it will deepen our understanding of what we get—and don't get—in a new home. Let's start with the entry sequence. Note we came through the front door. What difference does it make if you enter your home from the garage and pass through the laundry, as opposed to entering through the grand front door? One practical matter affecting either way of entering is the distance from the door to the kitchen. Entering a house through the garage has some advantages: it might make bringing in groceries and other items easier, or if you work or play outside, going directly from the garage by the laundry room allows you to shuck dirty clothes instead of dragging them through the house. Entering through the front door provides a different kind of experience: it is more about the transition from the outer world to your inner sanctum than about transporting items quickly.

Another factor that emerges when we look closely at the interior layout is the chance that sound from the second-floor area can penetrate downstairs to the first floor. If your children are in a raucous mood and you want to quietly read a magazine, you may be disturbed. Finally, in the Augusta, we see that the side porch off the entry foyer has limitations. If your property line is only five feet from your neighbor's lot and is marked by a fence, you will have very little to look at from your porch unless you provide some **clever landscape features** as a focus.

OPTIONS

Having looked with a critical eye at the model home as a whole, we need to understand the differences between the model home and the basic home. When you visit a **model home,** you are seeing a basic home that has been dressed up with all the extras—the standard floor plan with almost all of the available upgrades installed. The base price that you encounter in sales materials is often for the standard plan and no options. Your choice of options can dramatically increase your home's final price. Once again, this is a standard and expected marketing practice. A visit to a model home resembles a trip to an automobile dealer's showroom. You come in looking for a basic, no-frills model to fit within your budget. But all the cars you see have extras already added to them—flashy chrome wheels, racing stripes, extra technological features. The dealer won't remove those upgrades, and if you want a custom car (one without all the additional flash), you may have to wait months to get it.

The selection of options for a home works like customization on an automobile. If you don't want to buy a car available on a dealer's lot and instead order from the factory, then all your selections get added to a base price. It works the same way in choosing options for your home. For instance, in the Augusta model, you can add a fireplace to the living room or family room. You can choose to add an outdoor bathroom off the family room to serve as a changing room for swimmers if you add a pool. The lanai can be converted into an outdoor kitchen with a fireplace and

PRIORITIZING YOUR OPTIONS

Where do you really want to spend your money?

	PERFORMANCE	UPGRADES	COSMETIC
HIGH	Insulation (Consider higher R-value insulation)	Construction/Flex Options – Adding Floor Area	Flooring Materials
			Cabinets
	Windows (Consider energy efficient windows)	Appliance (Consider energy efficient appliance)	Countertops
			Bathroom Tile
	Exterior Façade – Roofing	Electrical – Exhaust Fan	Sinks
	Exterior Options – Moisture Barrier, Gutters	Plumbing – Tub/Shower	Garbage Disposal
		Garage Door	
	Plumbing – Exterior Hose Bibs	Electrical – Security	Ceiling Fan (pre-wiring)
	Plumbing – Toilet and Faucet (Consider water conserving and efficient plumbing system and fixtures)	Exterior Options – Landscape Sprinklers	Fireplace (depends on family needs, it could be higher or lower in this column)
		Electrical – Audio/Intercom	
		Construction/Flex Options – Adding Extra Bath (Depends on family needs, it could be higher or lower in this column)	Electrical – Cable and Telephone Jacks
	Exterior/Interior Lights (Consider energy efficient lighting system and bulbs, such as LEDs)		Painting/Drywall
			Trim Carpentry/Finish
		Room Conversions	Exterior Façade - Color and Veneers
	Air Conditioner (Consider efficient system)	Doors and Door Hardware	
			Exterior Options – Patio Covers, Deck Extensions
	Mechanical (Consider efficient water heater)		Tub/Shower Enclosure
	Exterior/Interior Outlets (ground fault breakers at all wet locations)		Mirrors
LOW			Window Treatments

Priority Meter

HIGH
Options that improve the **performance** of your house. Options that are harder to add and/or change later.

MEDIUM
Options that are important **"upgrades"** to your house. Options based on your personal discretions.

LOW
Options that are **cosmetic** or easier to change later. Options that can wait, or Do-It-Yourself afterward.

exterior grill. In the master bedroom, the large rectangular space can be subdivided by having a partial wall inserted in the middle so that the sleeping area is on one side and a so-called retreat is on the other. Often in this center element a television is located high above a fireplace; the angle of viewing seems a bit awkward, but the practice is widespread. All these options operate within the existing footprint of the building. The builder can easily provide them because he does not need to add to the foundation or floor slab.

Sometimes, adding doors that turn an open dining room to a study, or selecting an extra toilet, or adding a sunroom off the kitchen may make the house feel quite different from the standard model, even if the plan is much the same. Prioritize your selection of options and decide what counts most. You can always upgrade a carpet later, but adding a window is more difficult. Another factor to consider, even more basic, is whether you are more comfortable buying a cheaper house model and then adding many options, or buying a more expensive model and limiting your options.

Before you get to choose your options with KB Home, you must go through a few steps to confirm your serious interest in the house and your financial situation. As with many other building companies, a "sales counselor" works with you throughout the whole process. He or she is there to answer your questions so you could, for instance, confirm any details about the HOA in your neighborhood. After deciding on the model, the sales counselor will provide you with a purchase agreement, which includes the base price of the house, a description of the site, warranty information, and other legal disclosures. Upon signing the purchase agreement, you have to provide a deposit, also called **"earnest money,"** the amount of which depends on the subdivision. You must submit a credit application; your deposit will be refunded if you don't pass the credit check. After you pass the credit check, you are allowed to visit the KB Home Studio, the company's showroom, where you make the selections that finalize your house plans. Your final price is totaled to show all known costs, including your option selections.

THE SHOWROOM VISIT

Unlike KB Home, not all builders have their own showrooms, and some that do can be visited only by appointment. After visiting our model home at Fairway Estates and completing necessary paperwork, we head to a large, well-equipped showroom, the KB Home Studio. Though we have gone to a national **builder's showroom**, an alternative to the KB Home Studio, known as a builder showroom, exists in many locations. Your local builder may send you there to make the kinds of selections similar to those made at the KB Home Studio. Whether in a company-sponsored studio or a builder showroom, the main point is to see a wide array of brands for multiple products—hardware, appliances, carpet, roofing materials—in a single location.

At the KB Home Studio, located in a new office complex on the expanding northern edge of Austin, we meet a senior studio consultant. She is a consummate professional— experienced, knowledgeable about the entire line of product offerings, and committed to the company. She is also a highly experienced salesperson who knows how to steer home buyers through the range of options available.

Our studio consultant enters Fairway Estates into a computer, the model number for the Augusta plan, and the code for the specific elevation we selected. The computer then generates a complete list of all options along with the prices for each item; for the model we selected, an additional printout covers all available flooring materials. It should be noted that the prices are subject to change.

The range of options appears at first glance overwhelming. There are thirty-four studio option categories, ranging from small details, like exterior electric outlets, to large items, like appliances. With so many categories to choose from, the range is all encompassing. In fact, the individual items within each category are carefully selected and their numbers controlled. The exact criteria for including particular items rather than others are not made known, but popularity and efficiency are probably important factors. I asked our salesperson whether some items are featured over others because they produce a higher profit for KB Home. She insisted that the profit margin on, say, one style of tile is the same as on another, though of course the exact profit margin is a company secret.

The KB Home Studio is arranged to allow the shopper to view items in sequence, with the most important and most expensive items coming first. This arrangement prioritizes your purchases; it would be terrible to realize you had overshot your budget before selecting a refrigerator. Many of the products come from manufacturers whose brand names are well known. That kind of familiarity gives a shopper confidence. For the highest-end homes, another alternative exists at a different location, a luxury version of the showroom, but the Home Studio serves the needs of consumers in all other prices of the KB Home line, from the smallest and least expensive to the higher-priced models.

The printout is clearly and logically organized. It provides a guide to the options we will add to our basic house model. The categories focus on major divisions of construction upgrades, exterior options, interior options, exterior façade materials, and flooring materials. The items in the individual categories are catalogued in great detail: description, model number, color, and finish. Here is how it works. Let's use kitchen faucets as an example. Your basic model house comes with one Chateau Chrome single-handle kitchen faucet manufactured by Moen. An upgrade to Moen's

Aberdeen Oil Rubbed Bronze single-handle kitchen faucet with pullout spout will add $487 to your basic house costs. If that is what you want, you indicate the quantity of the item and add the amount to the running subtotal on the buyer's list.

In the Construction, or "Flex," category, you can add a "bonus room" on the second floor for an additional $8,500. This room is made by closing up the double-height entry space with a ceiling on the ground floor. The result adds instant square footage to your house. It is also a very profitable option for the builder, since all he needs to do is to add some additional floor joists, Sheetrock, and flooring materials into an existing space. Another Construction option is to choose a different bathroom look for an additional $3,080. For the kitchen, we can upgrade to the "Gourmet" level for $740, but upgraded appliances are not included. No other options are listed in the Construction category: if you want a particular shape to a room, or a combination of spaces that is not standard, then this streamlined process stops. A special request must be sent to the company for consideration and pricing, and sometimes the outcome of a nonstandard request is decided by the local contractor who is building the actual houses at the subdivision site. The builder's own priorities and scheduling concerns will come into play here.

In the category of **Exterior Options,** we see that getting the patio covered may cost an additional $9,836–$12,899, depending on whether the patio is extended or has a nook. An extended deck, measuring ten by twelve feet, as we might see in a souped-up model home, will cost an additional $2,900–$3,700. The decks are not sealed and so will weather in time; sealing them is either an additional cost or a do-it-yourself item. Gutters are not included in the basic model, but can be added for $3,018. Additionally, there is an option to have your house wrapped in Tyvek, a synthetic moisture barrier manufactured by DuPont, for $2,393. Since some sort of moisture barrier is always necessary in framed construction, a builder may use building paper, a version of tarpaper, for this purpose.

Already it should be clear that with the selection of at least some of these construction options, the price of your **basic model** has started to grow. The same kind of selection process applies to the **Interior Options.** Upgrades are available for the cabinets in every room, including the laundry. The same applies to countertops, with the range of prices varying considerably. While a standard laminate kitchen top may be included, selecting a high-end solid-surface Silestone counter could cost as much as $7,835. The number of available sink faucets is extensive, and the choice may seem arbitrary. But an area that calls out for an upgrade is the tub-shower combination. The basic unit is a very plain fiberglass tub-shower combination;

ANNOTATED OPTION LIST EXCERPTS

	Qty	Unit Price	Total
FAUCETS			
1 handle kitchen w/ pullout spout			
Camerist Stainless # 7545SL		$300	$_____
1 handle kitchen w/ pullout spout			
Castleby Chrome # 7905		$104	$_____
2 handle kitchen w/ matching finish side spray			
Castleby Stainless # 7905SL		$174	$_____
2 handle kitchen w/ matching finish side spray			
Chateau Brushed Chrome # 7434BC		$71	$_____
1 handle kitchen w/ matching finish Protégé spray			
Chateau Chrome # 7425			

showroom displays a dozen or so of the popular products, additional options would be shown to you in cutsheets

wide price range

options on faucets are over two pages long

PAINTING/DRYWALL-INT TRIM			
Paint			
Sherwin-Williams low-VOC paint, Swiss Coffee color		Included	$_____
Sherwin-Williams low-VOC paint, Color Upgrade		$2,245	$_____
Drywall			
Drywall - Rounded Corners		Included	$_____
EXCLUDES ALL WINDOW RETURNS			

a creamy white

this is important for your health

if you want your walls to be a cooler white, it will cost you

a separate marble tub and tile surround costs considerably more, and tub-shower enclosures are additional. (The bathroom is also one of the few areas that can be "converted," which in this case means extending the vanity sink and cabinet or raising them in height.)

As with faucets, a large range of options exists for **light fixtures.** This may be one of the more challenging areas of option selection: what you see is the object, but what you get is the light its bulb produces. The image of the light fixture comes before knowledge of its efficiency—and energy consumption by lighting is a long-term cost. The number of available light fixtures (for indoors and outdoors) varies, and can be as many as 140 different items. Multiple choices in finishes for the same fixture contribute to this number. The number of options may appear boggling, but having the actual fixtures in front of you—along with advice from the sales agent—helps. Lighting in general is an area that even in high-end homes, custom designed by architects, rarely reaches its potential to create not only effective illumination but also ambience and atmosphere. Lighting has a great impact on our mood and experience, but its implementation is inadequately understood.

Appliances are another well-stocked category, and there is a wide range of choices for electric ranges, cooktops, built-in ovens, dishwashers, microwave ovens, and venting hoods. In the standard agreement, you get a basic model along with some necessary appliances, but if you want a washer, dryer, or refrigerators from KB Home, you must add them to your base cost.

As we go through the showroom, we get an increasing sense that the builder has thought of almost all our needs, including interior items that might fall under the category of **interior decoration.** Options exist for ceiling fans as well as window treatments, presented here as blinds. Adding "Woodmates 2 inch" blinds by Hunter Douglas as a whole house package will add $5,030 to our base cost. At the same time, because we experience a model home as complete, we tend to assume that many elements are naturally included in a basic home, even for a larger model. Not so. While most model homes will feature at least one fireplace, they too are optional items. A basic package for a security system is included, but several additional items need to be added before you can take full advantage of it. Home entertainment, audio, and intercom systems are strictly optional, as is wiring for a home media network. In light of the importance of our automobiles and where they are stored, options are available for the garage door, lights, and interiors.

Some options may be more difficult to decide upon than others. Choosing **color schemes** is notoriously difficult. Anyone doing a bit of repainting has seen that color on a little sample chip and color on a wall may look very different. One standard color comes with the basic house—Swiss Coffee, a beige tone. If you don't like pale mocha everywhere, then a single-color upgrade will cost $2,245, but you will need to decide on that color for yourself.

Energy items are not identified as a separate category, but probably should be. Truly invisible, but probably a wise long-term investment, is an option to add insulation to walls and attics (R-15 insulation for walls and R-38 for the attic area). Perhaps in the future this kind of insulation will be part of the standard package as local codes increasingly require all construction to be energy efficient. Upgrades to air conditioners, along with extended warranties, are options—a premiere platinum package could cost $15,540 additional.

While some categories are overwhelming in the number of items offered, some are surprisingly small. **Window** options for this model allowed only three upgrades, including an "obscure" bath window. An ever-expanding range of glazing materials that reduce glare, ultraviolet-light penetration, and even sound is emerging from manufacturers. These options, which provide energy efficiency and increased comfort, are not available for the model under consideration.

But hose bibs, or exterior water faucets, are available and must be added to the perimeter of the home. Water softeners can also be selected.

BRIEF HISTORY

WALLPAPER

George Washington and Thomas Jefferson, drawing inspiration from the elite homes of British officials in the early American colonies, ordered wallpaper for their own homes. Jefferson, a budding amateur architect, became a trendsetter by introducing wallpaper into the American home. But the use of wallpaper was strictly for the wealthy, who could afford to import these papers from international sources. Because of the price limitation and the technical difficulties of affixing wallpaper to a surface, the use of it as an interior treatment went through ups and downs over the next century. Wallpaper reemerged during the Arts and Crafts movement (discussed later) in the mid-nineteenth century as a form of nostalgia for past interior decoration. Pattern and ornament books by Owen Jones and the architectural work of William Morris catered to this taste. The interest in wallpaper continued until World War I, when the war effort suppressed American "extravagance." Wallpaper materialized again in post-World War II America as the primary form of interior ornamentation in the austere, prefabricated homes created during the housing boom fueled by people affected by the war, including veterans and middle-class families. Many building companies, including Centex and Pulte, advertised wallpaper in late-1940s shelter magazines like Better Homes and Gardens and House Beautiful. But with the prospects of the Cold War in the mid-1950s, taste changed again toward reduced spending, and ongoing lifestyle choices caused wallpaper to lose favor.

Below: "Moresque Pattern" by Owen Jones, *Grammar of Ornament*, 1868

While most option items are predictable, there are some surprises. One is an option to have wiring for an electric-vehicle charging station, a wise anticipation of electric cars, which will become increasingly appealing to consumers. Also surprising is the option for Disney packages. Oriented toward children, these use figures and scenarios familiar to them: the Princess Palace package, a Revved-up Car Room, a Hannah Montana Hangout, and Pooh Corner. All these packages are available in "classic" or "magic" format.

Some options are available for the façades. The elevation for our selection includes a brick veneer treatment for the full front of the house, but upgrades in brick are available, and brick veneer can be added to two sides of the house. Some cream stone veneer is also included, and it can be upgraded on the front. In Texas, the exterior elevations can be upgraded with limestone veneer, a plentiful material, for an additional $8,334. A composition shingle roof, suggested to last twenty years, and a radiant barrier for thermal control are included in the basic model. If you choose to add a second bay, its roofing is additional. **Composition shingles** are among the least inexpensive and least durable of roofing materials, but they are the only choice available for this model.

Consistent with KB Home's overall approach, the Home Studio's offerings for **floor coverings** are extensive. From the samples, you select materials and decide in which rooms you want them. As the dimensions of every room and space are already known, the total square-footage cost is quickly computed. Of all floor coverings, **carpet** is often the least expensive selection. It can be applied over plywood decking, with less labor than wood parquet or stone tiles, and is often less expensive to manufacture. Carpet's low cost is one reason why it is so widely used in speculative housing or when cost cutting is a major consideration. Carpet, however, ranges broadly in quality and durability—it may wear out while a tile floor remains intact and serviceable.

Some choices of carpet can add considerably to our base cost: the Disney Center Stage Shag II wall-to-wall carpet costs $14,347; the same coverage by Newsletter would cost $1,693. Likewise, the cost of **laminate flooring,** made of glued-together wood products, has already been computed for each space separately. The Bruce Park Avenue laminate costs $248 for the butler's pantry and $1,597 for bedroom 5. The breakdown by room is very convenient, since it allows you easily to choose particular materials for different spaces—for example, carpet in all the bedrooms, tile everywhere else—and thereby prioritize your spending. The same procedure for laminates applies to tile flooring, which has the widest number of selections offered—over eighty in total—including many made of the same material but in different square sizes, with the larger-dimensioned tiles tending to be more expensive than the smaller ones. A vinyl tile option is offered, but limited to the entry, butler's pantry, kitchen and nook, and bathroom. It is the least expensive floor covering, but advances in its technology have made it more long lasting and more varied in color and pattern than its early twentieth-century versions. Apparently, you cannot have vinyl flooring in your dining room (or at least, KB won't install it). Finally, solid wood flooring is available in several species, including American oak, hickory, cherry, walnut, and maple. It can be selected in planks three or five inches wide.

After going through the showroom and finalizing the quantities and prices of all selected options, the total cost is computed. If the builder provides an **allowance,** it is subtracted from the price to make a net total. An allowance is an estimated amount of what an item may cost; it is the amount you plan to spend that is within your budget. For example, if you don't know the cost of your kitchen counter tops, your builder may suggest an estimated amount. If in making your final selection at the showroom, the cost exceeds the allowance, the new amount is entered in your budget and your overall project costs go up. If you go under your allowance, you may get a credit. After providing a deposit and signing off on the Options Selection worksheet, you are ready to finalize the cost of your dream home. The cost of all the options will be an addendum to your purchase agreement, and you must sign it at or before the closing of an escrow with the total price. An **escrow account** is an account at a financial institution for temporarily holding money. When the financing terms and agreements are in place, the construction phase of your dream home begins.

So what have we accomplished with our studio visit? What are the **pros and cons** of this system? There are so many decisions to make in building a home. But a home will feel like it's yours only if you make some of these decisions. The number of choices may appear bewildering. But we saw at the KB Home Studio that the process was clear and straightforward. In many instances, sample items showed exactly what you would get. The options are also limited. The disadvantage of limited choices is that the material or item you want might not be available, and it may be impossible to alter your floor plan or room configuration except at a large premium. The idea of **custom design** is heavily promoted by the building company, but that customization is carefully controlled. The **benefit of limits** is that it streamlines both your selection of options and the construction process. Few if any decisions will need to be made later during construction; that allows the builder to move swiftly, guaranteeing efficiency, profitability, and getting you a finished house as quickly as possible.

The highly efficient options-selection system tracks every item in a company's inventory and computes the cost and profit margin of every square foot of material, and this process is at the core of the building industry's extraordinary revenues. The base price of the home itself, as with a car purchase, may contain the least amount of profit for the builder. Lot sales, included with the base price, may contain a larger profit, but the options probably provide the most profit. I say "probably" because these figures are, understandably, confidential company secrets. Simple comparison shopping, however, makes this conclusion reasonable.

We can assume that a major building company like KB Home can buy all its products at massively reduced **wholesale prices,** much as Walmart or Home Depot does. Such deep discounts are not available to local builders—who can at least buy wholesale—or the consumer. The builder may even be able to dictate to the manufacturer certain specifications or to insist on large-scale production of specific items for their homes across the country. Even taking into account the high profitability of the add-on options, a building company like KB Home is still providing a dream home at a lower price than a fully designed house, custom designed by an architect. Economy of scale, for both labor and materials, rules the day, but what about the **intrinsic quality of your dream home,** its ability to create comfort and support your individual lifestyle?

Of course, as you leave the Home Studio, having chosen features and upgrades, you are not thinking about the builder's profit. You are relieved to have made so many decisions, and you are thinking about your dream home and how soon you will be able to move in to it. After the Home Studio visit and all decisions, including finalizing interior selections, have been completed, the construction permit applications will be submitted. Within a few weeks, you will meet with your construction manager to discuss the building process and hammer out any final details. Before construction begins, you should receive a **schedule,** a "Road Map," with a process time line, targets, and dates from start to finish. During construction, you should have the opportunity at various stages of the work to walk through and inspect the house with your builder. And your "sales counselor" should inform you about the meeting times. This gives you a chance to raise any questions or point out problems. Any changes would be discussed at that point, but the price (and design selections) should be fixed before construction begins in order for the budget to stay within the limits of your loan. Because you have picked finishes and options in advance, there should be few extra changes. No one wants delays, but many factors, such as bad weather or material shortages, or extra time needed to get permits and financing approval, could affect the completion date. Making changes to finalized orders has the potential to run up the cost of your house in ways you probably never expected or planned for. The exciting day arrives when the construction on your home is near completion and you are eager to move in. However, if you have not made previous arrangements, you will see that your yard and landscaping need attention. Regardless of how long that takes, your house has started to become your home. At KB Home, the anticipated construction time is four and a half to six months.

As your construction moves toward conclusion, you should start planning your move-in date. Besides moving your possessions, you may need to arrange for the installation of services such as cable television and Internet service. With advance planning, you can reduce the stress of moving. Finally, when construction is complete to your satisfaction and all your paperwork, including financing, is in order, you will receive the keys to your new home. Pay attention to the benefits, limitations, and durations of the **warranty** your builder provides you. Write down the anniversary date of your move-in as a reminder to see what, if anything, may need repair under warranty before then.

RECAP

TO-DO LIST

Right Before Construction

- **Meet with your construction manager and the crew if possible**
- **Request a schedule--a "Road Map" of the building process**
- **Review the schedule and ask questions**
- **Finalize the price *before* construction begins**

During Construction

- **Visit the construction of your dream home at various stages**

Right After Construction

- **Have a final "walk through" with your construction manager**
- **Plan landscaping for your lot (if it has not already been arranged)**
- **Make sure your financing is in order**
- **Know what the warranty provided by your builder will cover**

CASE STUDY 2: ROSE HILL

Let's look at another subdivision in a different part of the country: Rose Hill, a small community planned outside Asheville, North Carolina by a local developer (Fig. 23). The region is appealing for its access to the Smoky Mountains, Blue Ridge Parkway, relatively cool summers, and lovely views. Asheville is a city of 80,000 with much diversity and character, an arts scene, and a relaxed atmosphere. Although I found Rose Hill through the Internet, local residents could find out about it through print media also, including the newspaper and a weekly real estate flier in which the subdivision is featured. Couples without children and retirees appear to be the target audience, as seen in the developer's promotional materials. At Rose Hill, you can "Live Carefree" because the development is set up as a **condominium association**—though the houses are detached and on single lots—and the condo association, using your monthly dues, pays for lawn maintenance and provides other shared amenities, like a swimming pool, workout room, and tennis court. People tired of maintenance chores may find these services appealing.

The subdivision is twelve miles northwest of Asheville, and getting there requires driving along Patton Road, a highway with fast-food shops, auto dealers, and other utilitarian businesses on its sides. Eventually, you get to the village of Leicester. Beyond it and located in the country, the subdivision has created its own self-contained neighborhood.

The history of this hilltop as a site for development began when its original developer logged the oak trees that provided part of a forest covering. The next developer, who planned to call the site Rose Hill Plantation, cut down all remaining trees and modified the topography of the hill with heavy earthmovers to allow a ribbon of roads to be built perpendicular to the slope. He had an engineer lay out the roads and 103 building sites, and locate amenities, including a lake. He then built the roads, along with an infrastructure of drains, water wells for each lot, and a sewage system for the development. The roads, as named, are intended to create a bucolic atmosphere: Dreambird Drive, Regent Heights Road, Southern Way Lane, and Rose Creek Road. He installed a large structure that acts as a gatehouse to control access to the site, and a clubhouse that also serves as the current sales office for the development.

The developer failed, however, to move forward and went belly up; a bank assumed ownership. The current developers, Sulaski Tinsley Fine Homes, bought the

Fig. 23: Rose Hill neighborhood, Leicester, North Carolina.

distressed property around 2008. One of the company's principals, Mike Tinsley II, began his career in the late 1980s by working for Centex, one of the major national builders. Robert Sulaski, his partner, started out working on residential projects in Florida. The two began collaborating in the late 1990s on residential development ventures, founding their current company in 2005. They are general contractors and licensed real estate brokers. When they bought the land, they received a credit line from a bank and launched an effort to build houses on the site. I mention these details about successive developers, bankruptcies, and new owners because they may directly or indirectly affect the prices and quality of the houses built on these sites. There is no harm in knowing about the history of the land where your home will be built.

Instead of creating their own sales force as a large-scale builder might do, Sulaski Tinsley turned over the marketing of the property to a local real estate business with activities throughout western North Carolina. I met David Walsh from a local real estate agency at the development's community center, where he introduced me to the Rose Hill subdivision. He has been involved with real estate for

Fig. 24: Forsythia model home, Rose Hill.

several years and has a specialty in selling acreage. David is a broker associate, which means he is a broker affiliated with a sponsoring broker instead of running his own office.

The first item you see at the sales office, as we saw at Fairway Estates, is an overall site plan of the development showing the lots, trails, available sites, and sites built on; about a dozen lots had houses on them. Each lot is rectangular in shape and contains 0.16 acres, or 6,970 square feet. At that lot size, the smallest one-story house covers 20 percent of the lot. The rest of the lot is available, in principle, to the owner, but **covenants,** legally binding rules, control what can be built by the owners in their yards—for example, no jungle gyms are allowed here. Often covenants are used to control, among other things, the visual appearance of houses, with the intent to keep them similar. In mentioning the covenants, David made an observation that is assumed throughout the building industry: "As everybody knows, conformity is good for a neighborhood."

Our sales agent showed me six different models to choose from. The houses were represented by floor plans, but no elevations, and were named after plants, in keeping with the overall floral theme of Rose Hill: the Azalea, the Forsythia, the Evergreen, the Gardenia, and the Hydrangea. They ranged in size from 1,425 square feet on one level to 2,154 square feet for a house with two levels; some options allowed for lower-level basements as a way to increase the square footage. Presumably, any discussion about elevation would come up later, after selecting a floor plan.

We then toured the **Forsythia** model home (Fig. 24). At 1,505 square feet, the Forsythia had a compact plan with a foyer that led from the front door or the garage to an open kitchen with granite counter tops. The combined kitchen, dining area, and adjoining living area was the central focus of the house. Behind the dining area was the master bedroom (13 x 13 feet), along with master bathroom and walk-in closet. On the opposite side of the house and accessed from the foyer were two smaller bedrooms (12 x 10 feet), which shared a full bathroom. One of these rooms could serve as an office, the other as a guest room. From the front, the elevation is dominated by a two-car garage. The roof is pitched and covered with composite shingles.

If the Forsythia is built on a slope, there is the option of adding, with an increase to the base price, a stairway leading down to a family room, fourth bedroom, and storage and mechanical room; an optional porch and deck are also available for this lower level. Another option allows for a living room to be located off the first level.

In sum, this is a compact, tight, and efficient floor plan, roughly square in shape, that puts the master bedroom off the dining room, greatly diminishing its privacy. The second house I looked at with my amiable sales agent was the **Azalea,** which was built as a spec house for sale (Fig. 25). I noticed immediately the covered porch, accessed by a short run of steps. Built on a slope, it has a large, open first floor and covered porch over an extensive basement that tucks into the side of the hill. Because only the master bedroom and a second bedroom are on the first level, the open area containing the living room, dining room, kitchen, and nook felt more spacious than in the Forsythia. This spec house had just been leased to someone, who had an option to buy it. They would have choices about whether or how to finish out the lower level, which appeared in its basic state as open stud walls, open floor joists, and smooth, nicely laid, plain concrete-block walls. This house had a distinctly more open feeling to it than the Forsythia, and took advantage of the views. The steps leading from the garage into house, however, would be an inconvenience in bringing groceries or other items into the kitchen area.

Fig. 25: Azalea model home, Rose Hill.

Upon leaving the Azalea, I noticed that one of the few other occupied houses in the development resembled it, but had its garage flipped to the opposite side and used a different color scheme on the exterior. If conformity is a good thing, monotony is not. This flipping of elements in a floor plan is a standard way to vary designs in subdivisions in order to avoid monotony: aside from the garage being moved from one side to the other, the two houses were pretty much identical.

When I asked the sales agent where the plans came from and whether you could build from your own plan, he replied he didn't know where the developers had obtained the designs but that you had to stick to the six plans offered. In the sales office, I noticed a set of construction drawings—used in the actual building of a house—that came from a local architecture firm. When you shop for a house, ask where the designs came from. If they are just off the shelf, they may not have been made with your site and climate in mind.

THE PURCHASE PROCESS

Buying a house at Rose Hill involves procedures similar to those at KB Home. Step 1 involves touring the site, looking at a model home, and picking a plan—all with the help of a sales agent. Step 2 consists of a meeting with the builder or contractor to discuss any changes you might want, such as finishing out a basement or replacing windows with French doors off a terrace. The builder tells you if the changes are possible and what they will cost. Step 3 involves a visit to a showroom, often with personal recommendations by the contractor. You pick your finishes, appliances, floorings, and other items. The builder has given you an allowance for these items in the base price. If your selection goes over the allowance, the overall price goes up. Step 4 takes place when the price based on your selection is determined and you provide a 10 percent down payment at the signing of the construction contract. (Rose Hill's developer has a credit line with a bank, which allows him to proceed with only your down payment instead of a separate construction loan.) Step 5 marks the start of construction, which at Rose Hill will take four to five months depending on weather and other uncontrollable factors. Meanwhile, unless you are paying cash, you will have obtained your long-term mortgage through a bank, credit union, or mortgage department of the real estate brokerage. Step 6 takes place when construction is complete and you pay the remaining construction costs from your loan. Now you move in, start paying your mortgage and your condo fees, and enjoy living in the country. Even your lawn will be mowed for you.

Now let's look at some of the **pros and cons** of this subdivision. Base prices range from $255,000 to $357,000, according to the plan type. If we assume a negotiated purchase price of 10 percent off the base price (a reasonable reduction), we see the houses, including their lots, range from $161 a square foot for the smallest house (1,425 square feet) to $135 a square foot for the largest (2,380 square feet). It is immediately apparent that we get a better value for the bigger house. Onto these base prices we might add costs for adding unfinished spaces to the lower level; these cost $35–$59 a square foot. Since we are looking only at base prices, we will need to add on any items that exceed our original allowances or any other special changes we have requested from the contractor.

Making sense of the price requires comparisons with similar houses on similar sites. We can assume, however, that these houses are in the middle to high price range of similar tract housing. Their major appeal rests on the houses being relatively efficient and well built; on provided services that reduce or eliminate maintenance chores; on the availability of some community facilities; and on views of a lovely surrounding landscape. The current developer has a good reputation and appears capable of producing houses quickly and efficiently. The negatives reside less in the housing itself than in how the site was treated. All the trees were cut down, creating a barren effect and requiring the planting of new trees and landscaping to soften the openness of the hill. In the bare landscape, the houses seem lonely. The existence of landscaping is a big factor in the impact made by any model home. To show this clearly, we can compare a generic model home with landscaping to the same home, in an edited image, without it (Figs. 26–27). You will need to pay for additional landscaping for your own home at Rose Hill. The lots are minimum areas in an open countryside where most existing houses, including some visible at a nearby development, have larger lots. The side setbacks between the houses are also minimums, which means if the subdivision is fully built out, the houses may feel too close to one another. The open feeling of the countryside will be diminished by the proximity of your neighbors. Also, while the site has few houses built on it, your view could be compromised by a house built on the next street down the slope paralleling your house; the houses with the most secure views are the ones at the lowest level of the development, since probably nothing will be built in front of them. Finally, there are differences between the lifestyle claims and the reality. The existence of a community garden was not yet apparent, and the swimming pool at the community center is probably too small for the whole community.

We now have a grasp of the players involved, we have visited some typical subdivisions, and we are familiar with the process of selecting a house, picking out its accessories, getting it built, and moving in. Next, we will deepen our understanding of the house itself and the processes of designing, building, and selling by looking at a series of case studies taken from around the United States.

Figs. 26-27: Model home with (above) and without landscaping.

RECAP

THE PURCHASE PROCESS

A Basic Outline

STEP 1: **Tour the site**

STEP 2: **Meet builder to discuss plan options**

STEP 3: **Visit the showroom and select finishes**

STEP 4: **Sign construction contract and pay down payment**

STEP 5: **Start construction**

STEP 6: **Pay remaining construction cost as building finishes**

STEP 7: **Move in**

Start Planning Your Dream Home

PART III

A CLOSER LOOK

SITING

We are familiar with the players and the process of selecting and commissioning a home in a subdivision. We now will look more closely at a number of issues that affect the quality of your home and your experience of it. Specifically, we'll look in more detail at siting, design, and the concept of custom design.

Depending on availability, you have a choice regarding the lot you select for your house, but your builder or developer will have already determined both the **general siting conditions** and **orientation** of your new home. You will most likely not be able to ask that your house be oriented so that the front runs parallel the street. You should pay close to location of your lot with respect to sun in summer and winter, prevailing breezes, if any, and strong shadows that might fall on your home from large trees or other houses. The sun's path, local wind patterns, and even microclimates vary throughout the country—your location will have its own distinctive characteristics. Regardless of regional differences, sun, wind, and shadow will critically affect your enjoyment of your home, and they ought to figure in to your lot selection.

An ideal lot in the Northeast might allow a house to absorb winter sun from windows that open onto the south but have enough roof overhang, or a shading device, to prevent hot summer rays from penetrating deeply into the house. Too much unprotected exposure on the north should be avoided so that bitter winter cold can be minimized (FIG. 28). An ideal lot in the Southwest might also take advantage of winter sun coming from the south, but also allow for protection from the hot western sun that seems to hang in the sky long into the summer afternoon. Summer sun that penetrates a house heats upon surfaces, which in turns creates discomfort and runs up utility bills. On the other hand, lots continually in shadow, either from nearby structures or even trees, are also undesirable. Shade and shadow should be balanced for the most positive effects. You should have orientation, breezes, and shadows on your home-search checklist.

    I mention the ideal lot because not all lots are desirable. Typically, their layout represents the ways that subdivisions have been laid out for over a century and for houses of any scale. These techniques—laying out rectangular lots of minimal widths on feeder roads and **cul-de-sacs**—make it easier and more efficient for the builder to erect houses using standardized construction practices, something that

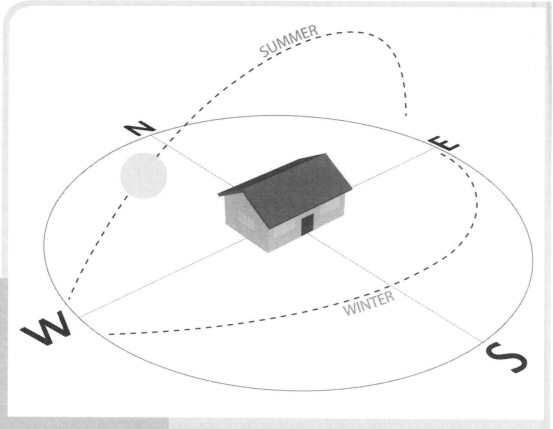

Fig. 28: House orientation and sunpath

saves him money and time. The advantages of a particular solar orientation are rarely considered. From the builder's perspective, individual houses with different orientations might require a distinct layout for each lot, a time-consuming process that adds to the expense of a house.

It sounds impractical to change the traditional system, but in the future our living conditions and environmental and energy problems may require rethinking how sites are oriented on subdivision lots. The means of taking advantage of sun and wind have existed for a long time—at least since the time of ancient Rome and the Renaissance. These are environmental issues, and while the building industry is highly sensitive to energy issues—it is busily incorporating energy-efficient products into its houses and proudly trumpeting Energy Star ratings—it barely has begun to explore energy-efficient layouts of neighborhoods and subdivisions, or the placement of houses on lots. While you are touring a model home and having discussions about modifications to your floor plan or your finish materials, your salesperson will probably not mention the benefits or detriments of the orientation of the house you are buying.

The problem of inappropriate siting occurs at all levels of the housing spectrum. In the Central Texas Hill Country where I live, I have often been amazed, even saddened, when I observe houses, from McMansions to entry-level houses, that have living rooms with big expanses of glass facing our withering western sun. From late spring to early fall, the sun seems to hang in the sky, and those rooms are often unusable without heavy curtains, besides causing utility bills to soar.

A woman came to see me to discuss a landscape design for her five-acre property. She wanted a plan that would take advantage of its trees, views, and terrain and would relate the site to her three-year-old house. The challenge, however, was her house, not the land. Although designed by a local architect, the house was placed so that the front door and high-ceilinged living room faced west, the direction of relentless summer sun; the heat and sun made the front of the house almost unusable. The views to the east, which gave the best access to some woods, a trail, and lovely overlook, were similarly ignored. So before the house could relate to the nature around it, the house itself needed some modifications that would filter unwanted sun and open blank walls where windows should have been placed. If the house had been more carefully oriented originally, the engaging of the landscape would have followed more easily.

Another issue related to siting that gets little discussion concerns the differences between building on **flat versus sloping sites.** The first Levittown was

FURTHER INFORMATION

ORIENTATION

*You may not have the choice now to change lots, but knowing what works and what doesn't is important, so let's review the issues. The arbitrary placing of a house facing the street means that it may not be taking advantage of the benefits of sunlight for warming an interior and for providing daylight. If a house is oriented to take advantage of the sun, it reaps the benefit of **passive solar heat gain**. When sunlight participates in warming our homes, we are saving energy and reducing our utility bills. Similarly, when sunlight illuminates the interiors of our homes, we don't need to turn on electric lights, thereby further saving energy and energy costs and creating a more sustainable lifestyle.*

In addition, the automatic placing of a house to face a street may mean that a house gets too much sun or none at all. In the warm months, a house facing the western, setting sun in the lower latitudes gets too much sun, and rooms become uncomfortably bright and overheated. In this condition, there is too much solar gain. To remedy this, we need to increase our air-conditioning to make hot rooms habitable, and that uses more energy and increases our utility bills. Also, we may need to add curtains or drapes to block or filter unwanted sun, which is another added expense. A house with a big picture window facing north may also add to energy costs. The larger area of glass allows more cold to penetrate in the winter season, possibly requiring additional heating.

These same kinds of siting issues may also arise when trying to take advantage of breezes that move over a site. With windows open during temperate times of the year, breezes may provide moderate cooling or heating effects that cost us nothing. Fresh air, when clean, also has health benefits.

Below: Diagrams showing wind flows around buildings at different roof pitches.

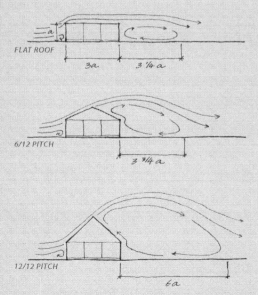

FLAT ROOF

3a   3 ¼ a

6/12 PITCH

3 ¾ a

12/12 PITCH

6a

Fig. 29: House built on a sloped site.

constructed on flat potato fields, and developers still look for flat terrain as their first choice for subdivisions. But in some areas, the convenient flat lands suitable for tract housing are already developed. Less desirable properties, then, are the only tracts available, and they may introduce problems that don't occur on flat sites. Standard practice, whether for large numbers of tract houses or single spec homes, is to assume that the lot is flat. When a builder buys a preexisting house plan from a plan factory, or when a company generates one from its design department, the design is made for a flat lot. The sole variation occurs with the possibility of adding a basement level.

We can see clearly in Fig. 29 what happens when a house designed for a flat lot is built on a sloping lot. In this instance, the builder has bought a large lot on the side of a big wooded hill that faces west. Beneath the thin layer of soil, the ground is mostly limestone. To fit the flat house on the sloped lot, he first excavated the side of the hill to a depth of fifteen or twenty feet. More land was removed at the foot of the cut to make a flat pad for part of the house. Tons of stones, dirt, and debris were trucked off the site and dumped elsewhere. The house was laid out on its pad with its back to the cut, but the front slope was left intact. Consequently, the living room and adjacent spaces ended up some fifteen feet above the existing grade below. As built, there was no means for getting from the main floor of the house to the land below it; the house sat stranded on a precipice. In principle, this might be a desired effect, but in this instance, with a tall exposed foundation in place, the living room appeared to float, as if it were severed from its natural location. Since this was a spec home, it was offered for sale during its construction process. It found no takers. While the house was still on the market, the builder than began trucking in thousands of cubic yards of fill material—stone and dirt—to raise the level of the sloping site up to the level of the living room. In normal construction processes, this huge mound of earth would need to be compacted and kept in place with retaining walls. As a result of using a design for a flat site on a steep hill, the builder had to spend money for excavating, trucking material off site, adding to the height of the foundation with retaining walls, trucking material back onto the site, compacting it, and adding more retaining walls. This added labor is expensive, and cost will be passed on to the buyer. It has also prolonged the construction process, which is an expense in itself. Finally, I should mention that this big spec house has its grand living room oriented directly facing the intense western sun.

SPACE AND PROPORTIONS

Another important, basic factor that gets little or no attention is how space and proportion affect the experience we have of our homes. Space is easy to talk about but difficult to define. We can remember certain spaces that we have loved, and we have favorite spaces, but explaining why one space is more appealing than another is challenging. Some rooms are used for specific purposes, like a home office, and others morph into multipurpose areas and places we move in and out of. But even when we move around at home with a laptop or notepad, we tend to pick particular spaces in which to use them. One way to discover the spaces you like is to ask what is your favorite space in your home now? How do you feel in this space? Is there anything in particular that makes you feel comfortable?

Measuring spaces that you like and recording those dimensions is a good technique for helping you prepare for the design phase of your dream home. Once on a Christmas holiday in Mexico, my wife and I were staying in a wonderful old walled resort in Cuernavaca. We had the good fortune to get a large room that opened onto a terrace. I immediately felt so at home in this room, which had a corner fireplace, that I wished I could take the feeling with me and transfer it elsewhere. My wife had a similar positive reaction. I thought that if I measured the room, I might capture some of its magic. Normally, as an architect, I travel with a little tape measure, but this time I had forgotten to bring it. With no other option, I took off my belt and measured the width as a number of belt lengths, the length as another number of belts, and finally I measured the height of the room from floor to ceiling. I put these measurements down in a notepad, along with a sketch as well as some indications of materials and the direction of light. It did not matter what I used to measure with, because it was the relationship of length to width to height that was central to my experience. The relationships between those dimensions defined the **proportions** in the room, and the proportions in turn made the space.

Proportion makes spaces have a psychological and physical impact on our senses. Like space itself, proportion is difficult to discuss. One way to get a better feel for proportions and their impact is to measure a room for yourself, as I did

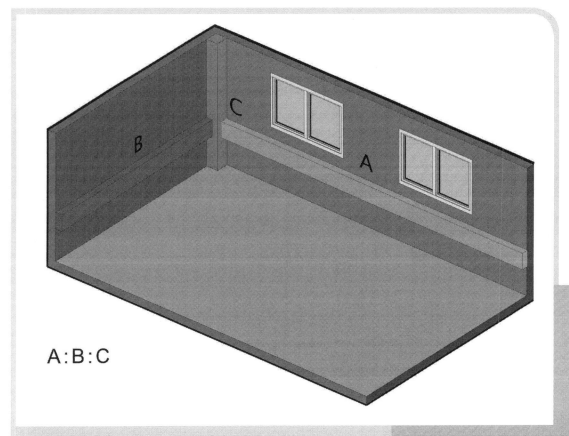

Fig. 30: Proportions of a room, length (A) to width (B) to height (C).

in Cuernavaca. You could pick your bedroom or the space that you have already determined is your favorite. Measure the length, width, and height from floor to ceiling and note down the dimensions. You will have three numbers that are related one to the other, length to width to height. This arrangement of measurements represents a ratio that defines the proportions of your space. Many effective spaces have simple proportions. A room that has a length-to-width ratio of 1 to 1 is a square. A room where the length is twice the width is 2 to 1. You can see how this works in the diagram above, where width, length, and height are labeled A, B, and C (Fig. 30). The relationship of width to length to height can be written as a mathematical expression such as 1:1:1 or 2:1:1, or, as in our diagram, with letters, where the proportion of length to width to height is given as A:B:C. Don't be thrown by the use of a few numbers—giving a math lesson is not my point. What is important to realize is that you can partly define spaces through the use of proportions and then use the proportions to obtain the pleasing special effects you desire.

The use of proportions has been a key means of creating beauty and harmony throughout the history of architecture, from ancient classical times in the West to building around the globe. Proportions, when applied to buildings, allow for control over the relationships of widths to lengths and even to heights. Over time, certain proportions seemed to create spaces that felt better, were more harmonious, and appeared beautiful, even if they were simple. Proportion is a basic means of achieving harmony.

Like good siting, the use of proportion in a home's design may have a beneficial, though subtle, effect on our experience. Many factors play into our experience of a home: color, the quality of light, the texture of materials, surfaces, acoustic conditions, and even smell. But the absence of good proportions is often a big factor in spaces feeling awkward. Conversely, when a space feels good to us, it is almost always well proportioned. Even if its designer did not consciously supply the needed dimensions, a well-proportioned space has a definable and often very simple ratio of length to width and even to height.

The presence or absence of harmonious proportions affects our reactions to the exteriors and interiors of the tract homes that interest us. On the exterior, proportions can play a role in the design of façades. Regardless of the specificity of details—for example, **a bracket versus a molding**—the proportional arrangement of elements can contribute to an overall pleasing effect. On the interior, we can immediately feel the relationship of width to height. When we look across the spectrum of housing types, we see that ceiling heights are a big factor in housing

BRIEF HISTORY

ANDREA PALLADIO

Andrea Palladio (1508–1580), a great figure of the Renaissance, was probably the most influential architect in the western world for centuries. His impact came partly from the fact that his designs were available in pattern books—precursors to plan factories and Internet providers—and that they were harmonious designs. The key to the beauty of his designs was his use of proportional systems, simple numerical relations. In discussing room sizes, he used 1:1, 3:4, 2:3, 3:5, and 1:2, and even added the numbers to his drawings so everyone, particularly builders, could understand their necessity. Now the important thing to remember is that **proportion can apply to any style:** *Palladio designed in a Renaissance classical style in the sixteenth century, but Le Corbusier, the great modern twentieth-century Franco-Swiss architect, also used proportional systems.*

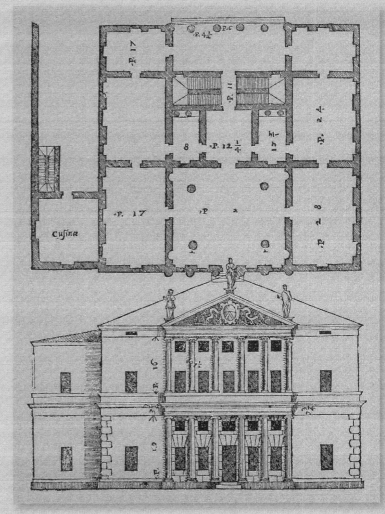

DEFINITION

*A **bracket** is a structural or decorative member that projects from a wall, usually to carry weight, or when used decoratively to emphasize a building corner. It is traditionally made out of stone, wood, or metal.*

*A **molding** is a strip of materials used to cover transitions between surfaces or for ornamentation. It is traditionally milled out of solid wood or cast in plaster. In recent years, it is common to find molding made from plastic, wood composites, or foam.*

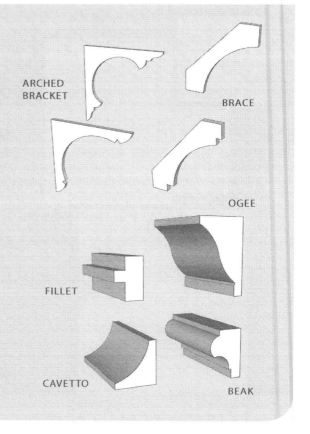

costs: High-end houses may have a ten-foot ceiling height for the first floor and nine feet for the second. Middle-level houses may have nine-foot ceilings on the first floor and eight on the second floor. And lower-priced homes usually have a maximum ceiling height of eight feet. The high ceiling of the more expensive house requires more materials and a bit more labor, something reflected in the overall cost. At the lower end of cost, materials and labor are kept to a minimum in order to keep the price low.

A remarkable factor that needs emphasis is that a room with a lower ceiling can feel comfortable when its width is proportional to its ceiling height. Conversely, a room with a high ceiling can feel unpleasant when the room is too narrow or too wide. A variation of the problem is seen when a low-ceilinged room is too wide to be comfortable. There are two points to remember here: any space, big or small, can feel good if it is well proportioned, and the use of proportion ought to be part of, and integral to, the design process, not an add-on costing extra. Being aware of proportion is another factor that will allow you to be perceptive when analyzing houses or model homes and to understand what works and does not work for you.

CUSTOM DESIGN

I mentioned "custom design" earlier, but it deserves a closer look. The term, or similar phrases suggesting that your new house will be special or unique, is a marketing tool that is gaining use as building companies increasingly rely on the Internet to introduce customers to their products and move them into and through the home-selection process. Conventionally, a custom-designed home is one that is specific to a client's particular needs. An architect or home designer draws up and specifies all the elements of the house in keeping with a list of needs decided on with the owner, from layout to materials and details. So-called custom design in the building industry is different: you are allowed to make certain selections, but only within a limited scope of choices predetermined by the builder. As we have seen, you get to pick a façade treatment, floor materials, hardware, bathroom fixtures, and appliances at the showroom, all of which must fit into an allowed budget or be added to your construction cost. Some options allow for the addition of a porch or basement, and some building companies' websites allow you to pick and choose items that you can assemble for your home. Many websites have a "design your own home" tool that allows you to put pieces and parts together from a preset number of options. It is quick and allows you to get a sense of possibilities. But these options are limited to those already provided by the builder. And the standard practice is that substantive architectural changes are discouraged, charged for at high rates, or simply not allowed.

For instance, suppose your hobby is astronomy and you want a small, special room for your telescope and a computer, and you want a portion of the roof to be retractable. The concept is reasonable and feasible, but outside the builder's frame of reference. You will be told no, that either you can't make such a change or that the cost will be exorbitant. The builder is set up to replicate houses by using standard methods and known materials, and to work according to his own schedule. Changes that require new designs, possibly additional foundation work, and new materials disrupt his work flow. They may slow down the construction schedule and could affect his profit on the products he is offering. Working within the given architectural constraints is the **tradeoff** you accept to get a house at the price you want and built within a short period of time.

What's important here is to understand that custom design means you get to make decisions about your home, but your home it is not the unique, one-of-a-kind object that the builder's promotional material may suggest.

THE SAME BUT DIFFERENT

This limitation brings us to the idea of **uniqueness** itself. A conventional criticism of suburbs is that all the houses look alike; they are cookie-cutter replicas stamped out by a system of mass production. Such criticism implies that the houses in suburbs are anonymous and by extension so are their residents. Usually, these kinds of comments are made by people who don't live in subdivisions, or by people who are championing their own agendas for the kind of design they want to impose on others. While it certainly is true that thousands of the tract homes built since World War II are virtually identical, they provided shelter and refuge and, often, a family's first entry into the housing market, a base from which to move forward and upward. They were elements in people's pursuit of the American dream. In addition, the automatic criticism of monotony in the suburbs fails to recognize that the building industry is currently providing more variety there than at any time in the past. In other words, when it comes to qualities of uniqueness in our housing, the situation is complex: variety and sameness coexist, and that has important implications for what we get when we buy a new home.

One fundamental trend in the housing industry is that the same house can have different names in different locations, and identical models can sell for different prices. Changing the name of a house can give the appearance of variety and also answer the criticism of boring repetition—even though the house is the same. Different prices for the same house in different locations reflect the costs of land, the state of infrastructure, and local demand. You may find your house reproduced on some other site around the country, and it will probably have a different name and a different price. **A second fundamental trend** in the building industry is to institute small changes to avoid monotony and expand the range of offerings. A relatively simple way to make the same house look different is to change the façade.

As we saw earlier during our site visits, we had a chance to pick from a variety of façades for a single house plan. This important option has always been part of stock plans, whether from plan factories or home builders, but the widespread availability of drafting software makes the fashioning of additional façades easier than ever and allows for amazing transportability. The transfer of façades—and plans—into digital formats is what is behind the choices on builders' websites. The ability to download in seconds premade plans means that anyone can have the design of a new house instantly, a process that might take months with an architect.

We can see an example of the same floor plan becoming a different house through a change of name and façade at Ryan Homes. The company, which began in 1948 in Pittsburgh, currently builds in metropolitan areas in the East and has constructed over 300,000 homes. It is now a subsidiary of NVR, Inc., a real estate development company that also owns NVHomes, Rymarc Homes, and Fox Ridge Homes. Two Ryan models, the Summerville (Fig. 31) and the Springbrook (Fig. 32), are the same house; the only differences are modifications to the gables, some changes to windows, and the addition of dormers in the Springbrook model. When we look at the floor plans, we see they are almost identical, with only one square foot of difference: 1,853 for the Summerville (Fig. 33) and 1,852 for the Springbrook (Fig. 34). The dining room of the Summerville has an octagonal tray ceiling, while the dining room of the Springbrook is square and has a flat ceiling. These same houses vary in price depending on location. In Simpsonville, South Carolina, the Summerville's cost is in the upper $160,000s; in Concord, North Carolina, it is priced in the upper $210,000s. Meanwhile, in Mars, Pennsylvania, the Springbrook is priced in the upper $410,000s, but in Greenwood, Indiana, its cost is in the upper $210,000s.

Thousands of examples reveal this process of making the same house and same façade appear different by altering minor exterior details and changing locations. Two other Ryan Homes models, the Brookmere for Simpsonville, South Carolina, and the Bridgeport, for locations in Virginia, sound like two different houses, but their only difference is a slight variation in the windows (Figs. 35 and 36). The façade of the Bridgeport has two separate windows in the living room, while the Brookmere has a single three-part window. The same kind of substitution is applied to the dining room. In the Bridgeport's ground floor, windows are capped with arches and shutters with curved tops; in the Brookmere, windows are flat topped, as are its shutters.

The floor plans for the Bridgeport and the Brookmere are the same except for minor optional changes (Figs. 37 and 38). Looking closely at the Bridgeport plan, you see the option of having a dining room that is rectangular with an optional tray ceiling, a front porch with four columns, and a three-car garage with entry from the side. In the Brookmere plan, we get a dining room that is approximately square, with an octagonal tray ceiling as an option, and a three-car garage that opens on the front of the façade. This change involving the garage doors has practical and visual implications. Having a side entry for three cars means that you need two garage doors and enough space to make a right turn into the garage from your driveway. That in turn requires a wide lot, and many lots are too narrow to allow a side entry. Consequently, seeing the garage on the front of the house creates an entirely

Fig. 31: Elevation, Summerville model home.

Fig. 32: Elevation, Springbrook model home.

different visual experience. In this version of the Bridgeport, three windows disguise the garage from the street; its looks as if there is just another room behind it. The illusion is that the house is bigger. In the Brookmere you are immediately aware of the presence of the garage door.

A variation of the Springbrook (Fig. 39) demonstrates a basic strategy for making nearly identical houses appear different; flipping the garage from one side to the other. It is pretty much the same house, with just a few minor façade changes. The intent is to create a sense of diversity and to avoid the monotonous visual impact that allowed critics to call tract homes "cookie-cutter" houses.

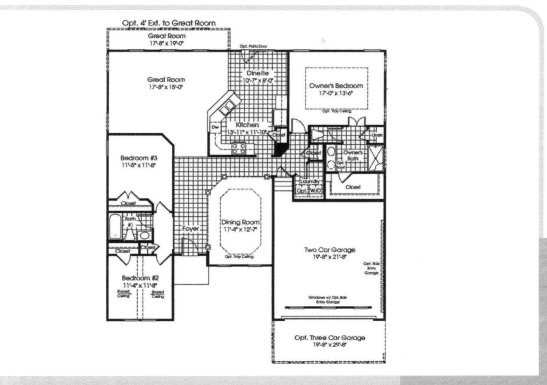

Fig. 33: Plan, Summerville model home.

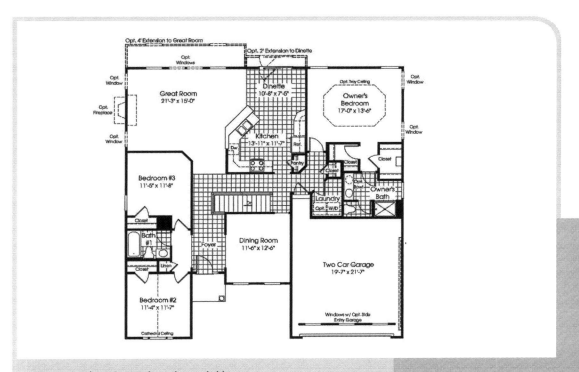

Fig. 34: Plan, Springbrook model home.

Fig. 35: Elevation, Brookmere model home.

Fig. 36: Elevation, Bridgeport model home.

There are hundreds, perhaps thousands of variations of these façade and plan types. If you look at a series of them, you will see that the general strategy for creating the appearance of difference comes from some simple devices, such as flipping the garage from one side of the house to the other, changing the façade and roof materials, and substituting a few exterior details. The interiors are virtually the same.

Finally, the same-but-different phenomenon is manifested not only in individual houses, particularly on their façades, but in the associations attached to the names of the houses. Ryan Homes, like many other big builders, produces variations by creating series with recognizable titles. There are references to

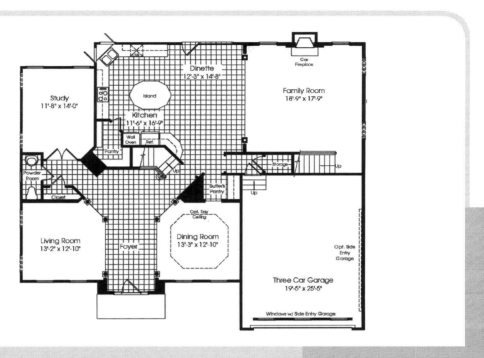

Fig. 37: Plan, Brookmere model home.

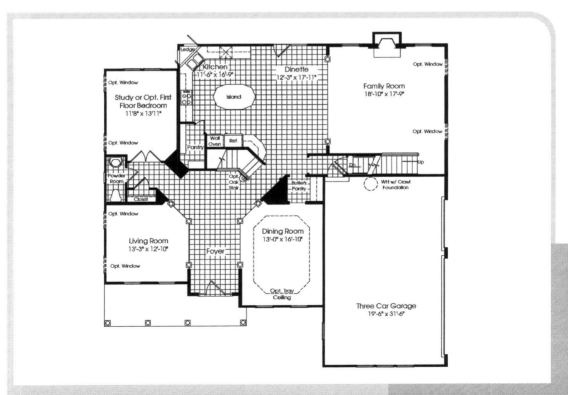

Fig. 38: Plan, Bridgeport model home.

Fig. 39: Elevation, Springbrook model home, with flipped garage.

Americana: the Jefferson model, which recalls Thomas Jefferson, a founding father, president, and talented amateur architect; the John Steinbeck model, a name recalling an author famous for capturing the lives of everyday Americans; and the James Michener model, which brings to mind big, multigenerational sagas happening around the globe. Even British authors can provide house names: the Keats model, which conjures up romance by linking the house to the Romantic English poet John Keats, and the Agatha Christie model, named for a writer whose mystery stories have made Hercule Poirot and Miss Jane Marple familiar to generations of readers and TV viewers. In addition, Ryan Homes has an extensive offering of models named after Italian cities: Florence, Pisa (a "renaissance-style ranch"), Rome, and so forth. They are offered in most of the states where Ryan Homes does business, from Delaware to Ohio. If we look behind the names, we see the same families of plan types repeated throughout these regions.

Next we will explore the subject of names themselves and what they signify about the housing industry and the identity of the homes in which we live. 🏠

PART IV

What's in a Name?

STYLES: A BRIEF HISTORY OF ARCHITECTURE

If you ask yourself why a builder would name a dozen of his American house models after Italian cities, you will not find a simple answer. It's true we love pizza and pasta, which we associate with Italy. Those of us fortunate enough to cherish memories of vacations to Italy can bask in the recall of its history, warm weather, and dolce vita (literally, "sweet life"). But the connection to Italy underlies one of the more fundamental trends in the housing industry: names are important when it comes to marketing homes, and the naming of homes and subdivisions reveals the role that themes play in the production, marketing, and classification of suburbs. The use of stylistic terms has been the traditional means of identifying our homes. Knowing something about architectural styles can help you evaluate the character of the dream home you are contemplating buying or building.

Although some of what follows may seem like a history lesson, my intention is not to put you back in the classroom. If you remember our discussion of the façades available for the Augusta model in Fairway Estates, one was called Country French. That name wasn't chosen at random; the designer or developer knew enough about architectural history to realize that certain features (windows with round tops, wooden shutters, stucco) could bring to mind a French vernacular building style, even though no house resembling the Augusta is likely to be found anywhere in rural France. The information in the following section is meant to help you make those sorts of connections for yourself.

We begin with a discussion of style. Style applies to several subjects. We say a woman has style when she conveys qualities that not only distinguish her from others, but also seem to resonate from some inner place. Princess Diana and Jackie Kennedy had such style. Artists are said to have individual styles when recognizable characteristics make their work different from others'. One artist's style might be defined by drips, another's by blocks of color. Architectural styles in the Western world have a more than two-thousand-year history, and during much of that time they were relatively straightforward and clearly recognizable. Although there were important historical precedents in the ancient Near East and ancient Egypt, the main story of architectural style begins with the classical styles of Greece and Rome.

Economic, political, religious, and social changes saw the classical tradition modified in medieval architecture, which is characterized by simplicity of overall

DEFINITION

CLASSICAL STYLE

The **Greeks** developed a beautiful architectural language using pediments (the triangular frame at the roof), columns (identified by their own stylistic subcategories), capitals (the caps of columns), and proportions. The **Romans** used the precedents of Greek architecture, added sophisticated technologies like vaulting and mechanical systems, and spread their architecture (and city planning) throughout the lands they conquered. Taken together, Roman and Greek architecture defined the classical styles that were emulated in various forms during the centuries that followed. The classical styles came to us in four versions known as orders: **Doric, Ionic, Corinthian,** and, later, **Tuscan.** Many famous public buildings in the United States are based on classical styles, including the U.S. Capitol and the Supreme Court Building.

Fig. 40: Detail, Church of St. Radegonde, Talmont-sur-Gironde (Charente-Maritime), France. Built in 1094.

arrangement (its massing), the frequent use of stone, and heavy load-bearing walls. A more specific term is **Romanesque** architecture, which, as the name implies, used forms found in Roman structures (Fig. 40). Romanesque buildings often lacked the complex features of the classical system, but nonetheless showed marked creativity. For example, masons invented their own artistic variations for columns and capitals.

The next major architectural style in the Western world was Gothic. Originating in twelfth-century France and lasting into the sixteenth century, **Gothic** architecture emerged as the product of technological innovations achieved through the use of pointed arches and buttressing (Fig. 41). (A buttress is a structure applied to an exterior wall to provide additional support.) These devices allowed for the construction of thinner and taller walls that could be filled with windows. The resulting dramatic soaring spaces, most often seen in cathedrals and other religious buildings, were unprecedented, and patrons often saw the vast, light-filled interiors as spiritually uplifting. The Italian **Renaissance,** beginning in the fifteenth century, saw a rebirth of classical ideas. Renaissance architects and artists who studied the ruins of ancient Rome saw classical principles as the highest achievement of human creativity. The Renaissance spread from Italy throughout Europe and became for over two centuries the preeminent style of architecture, leaving an indelible impact that

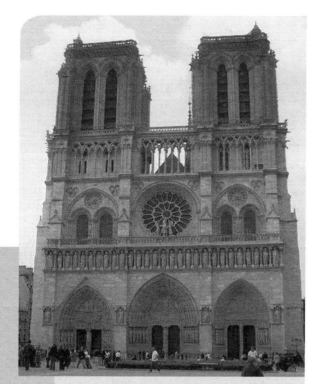

Fig. 41: Façade, Notre Dame de Paris, Paris. Construction started in 1163.

has lasted up to the present. The Renaissance set a trend for reviving an architectural style of the past but also transforming it according to defined rules. By the middle of the eighteenth century, late Renaissance architecture and its offshoot, the **Baroque,** still were rooted in ancient Rome. Greece was eventually seen as an even purer standard than Roman, and Greek architecture experienced a revival until the mid-nineteenth century.

The beginning of the nineteenth century saw variants of classical ideas give way to a bewildering number of revivals. Almost every style that could be identified in the past reappeared. Even Egyptian architecture was the subject of revival. While these revivals were happening, particularly in the later decades of the Victorian era (1837–1901), American architects and builders began to create variations on European styles, but also to produce styles that were rooted in the United States.

Revivals continued into the twentieth century. Previously revived styles appeared again as if for a second encore. But finally, trends that sought to be different and distinctly American started to emerge. For instance, from the 1890s to the mid-1930s, an American classical trend was revived, a variety of Italian Renaissance revival that had both urban and rural versions. During this period, Americans experienced the high points of the Beaux-Arts style, which had been absorbed by U.S. architects studying in France; the Chateauesque style; and English Revival. In the Southwest and California, new homes were designed in the Mission, Spanish Colonial, and Pueblo Revival styles. Following the earlier trend of styles becoming increasingly American, the Craftsman style, based on the Arts and Crafts style and Bungalow style, became widespread.

Three varieties of the English Revival style—Tudor, Elizabethan, and Jacobean—played a role in housing. An interpretation of early sixteenth- and

Fig. 42: Ralph Rollins House, Des Moines, Iowa, 1925.

seventeenth-century English manor houses, **Tudor** was conjured up by the use of masonry or stucco. The **Elizabethan** style relied on half-timbering (the imbedding of dark beams in white plastered walls). The **Jacobean** used shaped parapets. (It should be noted that all are often lumped together as Tudor.) In practice, houses in the English Revival style combined elements from each of these substyles. The key features, however, remain masonry, pediments shaped with curves, and half-timbering. Tudor was popular for large residences from the 1890s to the 1940s (Fig. 42). While examples of Tudor houses, from modest to grand, can be seen in many urban neighborhoods, the Tudor style is found rarely in models of the contemporary housing industry.

By the end of the nineteenth century, so many styles were competing for attention that it sparked a reaction to find a simpler architectural language, one that spoke to contemporary life, new developments in technology, and the perception that industrialization had changed every aspect of contemporary life. This was the dawn of the modern era. The desire to develop a clearly American architecture, as opposed to one obviously imported from Europe, found expression in the **Prairie Style,** best articulated by Frank Lloyd Wright and his circle in Chicago, along with other midwestern architects.

The image of the American home became the subject of extensive changes that began during the Great Depression and accelerated at the close of World War II, when returning veterans unleashed a huge pent-up demand for housing. Although Modern architecture had surfaced before the war, its impact was felt mainly from 1945 onward.

Modern style in the housing industry connotes a generic flat-roofed architecture, with lots of glass and flat walls—an image that contrasts dramatically with the pitched-roofed houses defined by traditional styles. There are no moldings on the interiors or exteriors, and no historical references. Some people feel that Modern is neither warm nor domestic.

This general image of Modern architecture has European origins. The relatively white, planar, flat-roofed architecture was seen as the emblem of the Modern movement, and its representative buildings had debuted in 1932 when pictures and models of them were exhibited in New York at the Museum of Modern Art. The organizers of the exhibition called this modern architecture the International Style—so named because its proponents hoped it would be used throughout the world. Americans saw a modern architecture that was stripped of

FURTHER INFORMATION

HENRY HOBSON RICHARDSON

Henry Hobson Richardson: The development of an American domestic style in the nineteenth century could be seen in the architecture of Henry Hobson Richardson (1838–1886). His work recalled Romanesque architecture, but had its own character, including the "shingle style," which featured a readily available material— the wooden shingle—to mark it.

Fig. 43: Bauhaus, Dessau Germany, 1925–1926.

any political and social intentions, being instead presented in formal, abstract terms. Those seeking to be on the cutting edge embraced it as the newest style.

Over time, the terms "International Style" and *"Bauhaus style"* became used interchangeably. The Bauhaus was a German school begun in 1919 with a focus on training designers in various fields to create objects that could be adapted for mass production by German industries (Fig. 43). It was not a school of architecture, although architecture was considered an ultimate objective. Instead of inventing a unique style of architecture, the teachers and students at the Bauhaus drew on other leading elements of modern design.

The Bauhaus put the aesthetics of these artistic developments to use in designing everything from teapots to weavings to metal tube chairs. The school eventually produced architectural designs, through collective teamwork, notably the school's building in Dessau, Germany, as well as a series of houses for the Bauhaus master teachers (Fig. 44). Those houses in particular captured the prevailing style, which got handed down: flat roofs, plenty of glass, and thin walls appearing as floating planes. But using "Bauhaus style" to describe all flat-roofed, glass-covered, abstract buildings is misleading.

Fig. 44: Haus Feininger, Masters' house, Bauhaus, Dessau, Germany.

FURTHER INFORMATION

SOURCES OF THE BAUHAUS

*The Bauhaus did not invent a style of architecture. Its sources were the modern movements in Holland, which in the late 1910s developed a pure abstract language using planes asymmetrically arranged and called **de Stijl** (the Style). Russia's contribution was a vibrant "Constructivist" phase in the same period that featured inventive imagery and dynamic, richly colored shapes. The innovative work of the young Franco-Swiss architect, Le Corbusier, who was re-thinking the basics of construction in terms of simple, rational building methods and new materials, particularly reinforced concrete, influenced all his progressive contemporaries.*

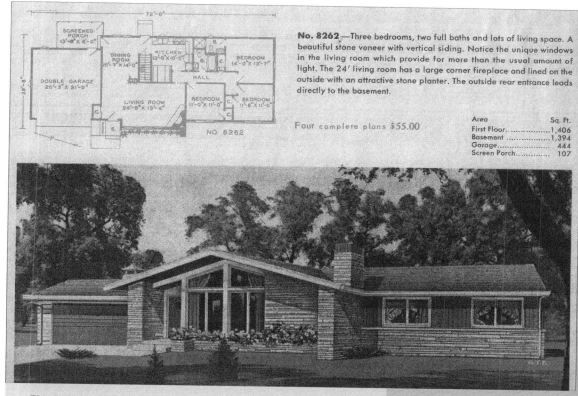

No. 8262—Three bedrooms, two full baths and lots of living space. A beautiful stone veneer with vertical siding. Notice the unique windows in the living room which provide for more than the usual amount of light. The 24' living room has a large corner fireplace and lined on the outside with an attractive stone planter. The outside rear entrance leads directly to the basement.

Four complete plans $55.00

Area	Sq. Ft.
First Floor	1,406
Basement	1,394
Garage	444
Screen Porch	107

Fig. 45: Model home no.8262, by Jarret Magbee. © The Garlinghouse Company

In fact, modernist, planar, flat-roofed architecture never became widespread in the American housing industry. A fresh response to midcentury modern conditions in America that did catch on with builders and the public was the **ranch-style home,** a single-story structure first popularized in the mid-1940s (Fig. 45). Drawing on a range of sources—including traditional pitched-roof models, the innovative middle-class homes by Frank Lloyd Wright that he called **Usonian,** and some of the aesthetics of the International Style—American designers began to produce efficient houses that responded particularly to climate and the real lifestyles of people. "Ranches" feature a gable or hip roof (one in which all sides of the roof slope downward toward the walls), an elongated floor plan with public rooms opening on to one another, and a long hallway from which bedrooms and bathrooms are accessed. The split-level, or "raised ranch," is a variation that gives the appearance of a two-story home. Actually, the ground floor is built partially below grade, though higher than a basement, and a second floor is added. It was popular, flexible, and efficient to construct. It varied in quality, but lost its importance as a model for the building industry as more traditional images began to replace it from the late 1970s onward.

FURTHER INFORMATION

USONIAN HOMES

*With his philosophy of organic architecture, the American architect Frank Lloyd Wright (1867–1959) regenerated the concept of the **American suburban home.** Rather than continue borrowing imported European styles, Wright wanted to develop a uniquely American idiom. It first emerged in his early Prairie period that culminated in 1910. His interest in housing for the middle class never flagged, and in the late 1930s, he began to develop what became known as the "Usonian" concept. Usonian homes were usually single-story, modestly sized houses that middle-class families could afford. Basic features included low cantilevered roofs, open living spaces, heated floor slabs, carports, and work spaces instead of kitchens. Like his earlier work, they emphasized the use of natural materials to evoke the surrounding landscape and create design connections between indoor and outdoor spaces. From 1945 to the 1960s, Wright's Usonian architecture played a vital role in the proliferation of ranch-style housing.*

Below: Jacobs House, 1936, Madison, Wisconsin.

THE STYLES ADAPTED TO HOUSING: THEN VERSUS NOW

It is important to note that when the styles of architecture discussed above dominated construction, they were applied to a limited range of building types: religious buildings like cathedrals, civic and cultural buildings, palaces, and grand homes for the ruling classes. Everyone else lived in whatever shelter they could afford. Housing structures for ordinary folk often expressed social standing as well as local building practices and materials. Building styles derived from local conditions without reference to the grand styles are called **vernacular,** the style of the people.

Vernacular houses responded to their environments. The **New England Salt Box** answered the demands of the climate and an economical lifestyle by having two stories in the front and one at the rear, with a sloping roof covering all (Fig. 46). It used simple wood framing for its construction. A house could start as two rooms on two floors and then expand to add a third room at the rear. The name comes from the dwelling's resemblance to a wooden box that held salt. Adobe mud bricks and flat roofs made sense in New Mexico, where the walls could trap the heat and little

Fig. 46: Vernacular style, Russell Potter House, Providence, Rhode Island, 1813.

Fig. 47: House with bark front, Athapascan Native American, Alaska, c. 1904. University of Washington Libraries, Special Collections (NA 2947).

Fig. 48: Dogtrot house, Dubach, Louisiana.

rain fell. In the Pacific Northwest, homes needed pitched roofs to shed the persistent rains; they also took advantage of the abundance of timber in the region and had a long tradition in the shelters of native Americans (Fig. 47). Popular in many southern states, the dogtrot house had two basic rooms separated by an open corridor, which allowed breezes to flow through, the whole structure covered by a single pitched roof (Fig. 48). In areas where wood was in short supply, pitched metal roofs allowed dogtrots to shed water from the occasional downpour. Vernacular architecture was regional by definition. As the housing industry developed, vernacular designs lost ground to styles that were applied across many regions, regardless of the local conditions that had originally made the vernacular special.

Now we move from the general categories of major architectural styles to look more specifically at the styles applied to American homes over time and at how they have migrated into the stock of builder housing. Quickly, we see that there is a great deal of variation in home styles, depending on region, climate, materials, and customs. The abundance of variations may seem daunting, but fortunately there are guides, both printed and on the Web, that allow us to navigate among the examples of this rich heritage (see Sources). Looking at historic houses and thinking about how they relate to your own preferences may be both fun and a great way of deepening a sense of the history of our country. The history of houses—and their styles—is a testament to American history. From slave quarters to grand mansions, they can tell us who we were and maybe where we are going. As we focus on styles that found their way in one form or another into the housing production system, we will consider what they looked like when they originated and how they are interpreted now.

Colonial Style

The term **Colonial architecture** is most accurate when it refers to houses built in North America from the arrival of the first European settlers in the early 1600s to 1776, the year of national independence. It overlapped and was derived in part from the **Georgian style** in England, and sometimes the terms are combined as Georgian Colonial.

Most styles are identified by their details. A Georgian Colonial style house can be identified by major elements: an entry with an arched opening, three-part windows with a central arch, keystone, and entablature (the horizontal moldings and bands above column capitals), and cornices with small blocks called modillions (Fig. 49).

The general model for colonial architecture, encompassing early colonial and Georgian styles, featured symmetrical floor plans and exteriors, which were meant to produce a dignified and orderly effect. The corners of the house had quoins (pronounced "coins"), which were blocks regularly alternating in size at the edges of the building; they recalled the idea of stones reinforcing the corners of a building, but in practice could be simple applied panels that supplied the idea and image of structural support without actually providing it.

After 1776, a preference for moldings, the lighter treatment of entries, and details based on work of the Adam brothers in England led to houses being built in the **Adam style.** Also known as the **Federal style,** it confirmed the growth of our fledgling national government. The Adamesque-Federal style emphasized Roman architecture, details, and at times a light treatment, particularly in interiors. The style's spread coincided with the emergence of architects and pattern books, which were the ancestors of house-plan catalogues and e-plans. In ordinary use, the terms "Colonial," "Georgian," and "Federal" are often applied interchangeably.

The Adamesque or Federal style can be seen clearly in the George Read II House in New Castle, Delaware, of 1801 (Fig. 50). We immediately notice the materials: brick instead of wood for the façade. The bricks visually contrast with lighter painted details, which include an elaborated entablature over each window, with a keystone at its center. The entry is marked by an arch and a fanlight, and above it on the second floor is a three-part window with an arched center. The overall proportions of the house,

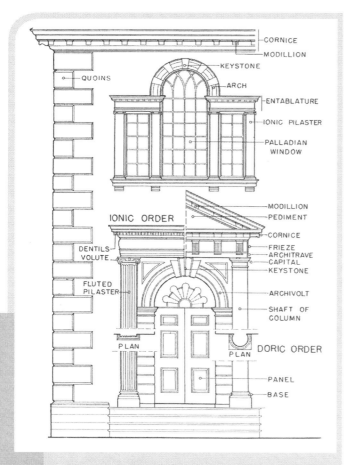

Fig. 49: Georgian details.

as well the proportions of the windows and dormers, accentuate the verticality of the design. Beyond any details, that verticality plays a big role in our response to the building as something elegant. A house built by Edward Pearsall in 1825 in Tuscumbia, Alabama, further demonstrates the basics of the style: symmetrical organization, a flat front façade, multi-paned windows that are flat topped and flanked by shutters, a pitched roof with gables on the short end, and a simple color scheme of white and dark gray for details (Fig. 51). The proportions balance the horizontal and vertical elements, so the effect is pleasing to the eye.

Other styles became more popular after 1820, but the American centennial of 1876 directed a lot of attention to our country's origins, and with that interest arose the **Colonial Revival.** Even as other styles competed with it and superseded its dominance, skillful architects still used the Colonial style to

Fig. 50: Federal style, George Read II House, New Castle, Delaware, 1801.

Fig. 51: Federal style, built by Edward Pearsall, Tuscumbia, Alabama, 1825.

advantage in the first decades of the twentieth century. We can see in an unidentified house built in Denver around 1900 the adept use of proportion and a careful control of detail that provided grandeur and status for an obviously prominent Denver citizen (Fig. 52). The windows, dormers, porch, brick, and paired chimneys identify it as a revival, yet the inventive combination of blind panels (flat surfaces without openings) and round-headed arches demonstrates finesse and skill. By the 1920s, the Colonial style could be purchased in an economical model, as seen in an English colonial from the pages of the Sears, Roebuck and Company House Catalogue of

FURTHER INFORMATION

WAYS OF LOOKING

One way to look at the styles of American homes is to look at them by region. In the **colonial traditions,** we see New England types that begin around 1620 as simple one- and two-room English cottages, two-story Salt Boxes, Cape Cod Cottages, Rhode Island "Stone-Enders" and a particular New England Georgian style. In the Hudson River valley, we find distinctive brick and stone farmhouses. In the mid-Atlantic and Upland South, houses with Quaker plans and those with Continental plans emerge in addition to mid-Atlantic Georgian and log-built houses. These kinds of proliferations appear in the Chesapeake Bay Tidewater, the Southern Tidewater, the French Mississippi with its Creole style cottages, plantations, and townhouses, and the Spanish colonial styles beginning as early as 1600 with concentrations in the New Mexico Territory and California. The popularity of these styles varied; some were used for short periods of time, others had long lives that continue to the present.

Another way to look at American homes is to look at them by stylistic categories. Some historians have noted that colonial houses in America built from 1600 to 1820 could fit into seven categories: post medieval, English, Dutch colonial, French colonial, Spanish colonial, Georgian, Adam, and early Classical Revival.

Fig. 52: Colonial Revival style, unidentified residence exterior, Denver, Colorado. L.C. McClure, photographer, c. 1900.

1929 (Fig. 53). The seven-room, two-story model has all its pieces and parts precut and ready for shipping to your site for $4,030. It is more faithful to the Colonial style than the Edward Pearsall house of 1825, featuring the elements of the style and the appropriate proportions. The Sears model, however, makes an adjustment at the entry, where the pediment is arched instead of flat on the bottom.

Easy recognition of the Colonial style, however, became more difficult during the Depression and World War II. Vastly simplified versions of the Colonial style appeared, as we see in an example from 1940 designed by Schreier & Patterson, architects for a subdivision called Woodacres VII in Montgomery County, Maryland (Fig. 54). The looming war produced a scarcity of building materials, but the big changes here concern proportion and detail. In this economical house, elimination of the cornice and the replacement of columns at the entry with posts completely alters

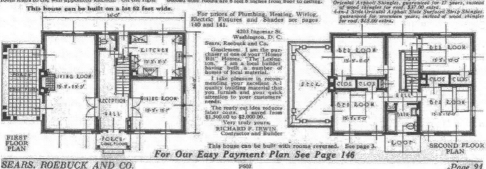

Fig. 53: Colonial Revival style, the Lexington model, *Honor Bilt Modern Homes*, Sears, Roebuck, and Co., 1929.

Fig. 54: Colonial Revival style, Woodacres VII, Maryland, Schreier & Patterson, architects, c.1940.

the sense of the house being in the tradition of the Colonial style. Economic necessity drove these changes: instead of allowing some space between the upper windows and the roof, the builders have set the roof structure on top of the upper-story windows in order to save material. The shutters have been retained as vestiges of the style and as a visual sign that this is a residence.

Despite the emergence of competing styles, the Colonial style remained available in the housing market. But the image of what defines the Colonial has changed dramatically. A home identified by the housing industry in 2012 as being in the Colonial style is vastly different from what preceded it (Fig. 55). This plan, obtainable from a plan-provider website, shows a house that is asymmetrically arranged instead of symmetrically organized as in a Colonial precedent, and has steep, tall, hip roofs instead of a gable-ended or flat roof. The proportions of the

Fig. 55: Colonial Revival style, Eplans.com house design no.HWEPL00880, 2012.

Fig. 56: Colonial Revival style, unidentified house, Austin, Texas, 2012.

double-height entry are out of sync with the rest of the front façade, which visually moves up and down without the uniformity and order found in Colonial styles. The "Colonial" elements are intended to be present in the pediment gables, the arched windows, and the columns topped with pieces of cornices. The same approach can be seen in a home recently built in Texas: on the front façade there are lintels with keystones, an oval window in the gable, shutters, moldings, cornice returns, and a triple window (Fig. 56). Brick is used as façade veneer, and it has washes of white on it to give an aged feeling. But the asymmetry of the overall massing of the house, the steep pitch of the roof, the combination of roof shapes with gables, and the double-height arched entry create an effect that differs dramatically from the quieter symmetry and order of earlier Colonial models.

Chateau Style

When wealthy Americans visiting Europe in the nineteenth century saw the amazing chateaux of sixteenth-century France, they wanted the style replicated in their own Chateauesque mansions, which sprang up in major East Coast cities, Chicago, St. Louis, and elsewhere. To accomplish such designs, young American architects began studying in Paris at the **École des Beaux-Arts** and paying attention to these grand monuments to wealth and power, either by visiting the buildings or studying (and borrowing) their details from widely available picture books and folios. The style, as translated, featured tall decorated chimneys, ornate dormer windows with complex moldings, "hooded" frames over windows, and often a recessed entry. Steep pitched roofs and the use of masonry also characterized the style, as did circular towers. The features, which had origins in medieval fortifications, were often highly elaborated, particularly in the pointed roofs. The Hecker-Smiley Mansion in Detroit conveys their impact (Fig. 57). Generations of wealthy people assumed that if the style was good enough for the Vanderbilts, it was good enough for them. Financial success—and all that it brings—has always been associated with this style. So it is not surprising to find versions of it being designed during the boom years of the 1990s and early 2000s (Fig. 58). The translation of the Chateau style into large homes included some of the key elements of original chateaux, such as turrets with conical roofs and detailed chimneys, but the replacement of surface materials, such as stucco over wood framing instead of stone, created a very different impression. The Detroit mansion looks massive, heavy, and solid, while the contemporary version appears as a light screen, its surface perforated with multiple windows.

Fig. 57: Medieval Chateau style, Hecker-Smiley Mansion, Detroit, Michigan; Louis Kamper, architect, 1889–1892.

Fig. 58: Chateau style, gated chateau, Austin, Texas, c. 2006.

Victorian Style

Of the wide range of styles that emerged in the Victorian era, some were seen collectively as **Victorian style,** a term that reduces distinctions between individual approaches but still brings to mind a generalized image. We will look at only a few of the separate styles that made up Victorian style. **Mansard style,** for example, can be identified by its curving treatment of the attic roof. The **Stick style** combined a half-timber image that looked like "sticks" with high steeped roofs, large brackets, and tall proportions. This widely used style could have complex details in its eaves and balustrades, giving it a gingerbread effect. The **Queen Anne style** was noted for its corner turrets, irregular plans, and variety in colors and surface treatments. We can see some of these features nicely in the Cohen House, Sheffield, Alabama (1896), with its turned columns on the veranda and second floor porch, elaborately pierced banding (woodwork), corner turret treated as a partial octagon, color variety,

Fig. 59: Victorian style, Annie and Bartow Cohen Home, Sheffield, Alabama, 1896.

Fig. 60: Victorian style, home in Hampstead, North Carolina, c. 2010.

Fig. 61: Craftsman style, Elsmore model, Honor Bilt Modern Homes, Sears, Roebuck, and Co., 1916.

Fig. 62: Craftsman style bungalow, Des Moines, Iowa, c.1920

Fig. 63: Craftsman style home by Pulte Homes, Richmond, Washington, 2012.

multiple textures, and overall asymmetrical arrangement (Fig. 59). The Victorian style remains popular today, as shown in this home in Hampstead, North Carolina (Fig. 60). When the style is used in housing now, it is often produced by a spec builder or built from predesigned plans purchased for local construction. Though it might be offered as a high-end house, the elaborate detail that defines the style makes it much less prominent in the standard offerings of the big builders. The industry needs simpler styles if it is to produce its houses quickly and efficiently.

Arts and Crafts Style

In mid-nineteenth-century England, problems arose from industrialization. People who used to make things by hand saw their skills and jobs taken over by machines. Industry disconnected people from the ways they had earned their livelihoods for generations, and that disruption had unsettling social consequences. In response, a reform movement arose to bring back the art and craft of design to the individual worker, to use materials in truthful ways according to their real properties, to emulate nature, and to simplify all aspects of life. The **Arts and Crafts** movement spread broadly and had a large number of followers in the United States, where it came to be called **Craftsman style** (Fig. 61). By the late nineteenth century, Arts and Crafts elements could be found not only in architecture but also in furnishings, including rugs, windows, and ceramics. Notable features of the style include the extensive use of wood, brackets under roof eaves, blocky proportions, wooden columns at porch entries, and built-in furniture such as buffets and bookshelves. In size, an Arts and Crafts house resembled the **Bungalow,** a style borrowed from the houses designed for British use in colonial India and specifically suited for warm weather. (The term "bungalow" derives from the Bengali "bangla," "dwelling.") Modern versions of the bungalow style are one-and-half stories generally and have hip roofs that provide large attic spaces and a place for heat to escape the main living quarters. The windows are grouped together to increase light and ventilation, and overhangs are broad to shade the house from excessive heat, as seen in this example from 1920 built in Des Moines, Iowa (Fig. 62). Both Arts and Crafts and Bungalow styles were widely used in domestic architecture and entered, with variations, into the stock of the building industry.

The Craftsman style still has currency among some of the big builders, as seen in a Pulte Homes' model home for Richmond, Washington (Fig. 63). It has the standard elements of roof gables, timber brackets, siding, and columns. One reason the style works for contemporary use is its simplicity. It provides a standard boxlike house with a pitched roof. Another reason the Craftsman style has broad appeal is its woodsy feel—the style is particularly appropriate for regions like the Pacific Northwest, where forests are abundant. The major difference in plan between the Des Moines version of 1920 and Richmond version of 2012 is the inclusion of the garage as part of the house. In 1920, a single car was stored in a detached shelter at the far end of the lot; in 2012, a two-car garage is set much closer to the street.

Mission Revival, Pueblo Revival, and Spanish Colonial Revival Styles

Three revival styles with roots in the Southwest and California continue to play a role in contemporary housing production. **Mission Revival** architecture, beginning around 1890 and reaching maximum popularity around 1920, recalled the Spanish missions built in colonial times in what would become Arizona, California, New Mexico, and Texas. It varied in form but often was two-story and blocky, with a low-pitched tiled roof and shaped parapets. These curving parapet elements are distinctive (Fig. 64). In some variants, a bell tower or pavilion, and wraparound porches with arched openings were part of the design. They were often made of stucco over lath (wooden supports)

Fig. 64: Mission Revival style, McCamy House, Dalton, Georgia, 1907.

and had white or light-colored walls. The style gained popularity after being featured at the Chicago Columbian Exposition of 1893, and its use in tourist destinations—hotels and resorts—spread along the rail lines of the Santa Fe and Southern Pacific railroads.

The Indian pueblos of the Rio Grande Valley in New Mexico, still occupied by ancient tribes, could be seen by tourists and others, and adobe homes, both in pueblos and in places like Santa Fe, provided stylistic models for revival (Fig. 65). By relying on traditional construction methods, in which skinned tree trunks support flat dirt roofs and materials on site are used for walls and floors, residents could expand their homes simply by adding one mud-brick or rubble-stone room onto another. The **Pueblo Revival style,** whether identified with New Mexico or the northern Mexican state of Sonora, is a style still produced by the building industry (Fig. 66).

Spanish Colonial Revival style surpassed Mission style in popularity in 1915 when the California Building at the Panama-Pacific International Exhibition created a positive stir. The style was ornate, with carvings around doors and windows, and featured a low-pitched red-tile roof with wide overhangs, and walls often of white plaster over brick or block. The style could be more restrained, as seen in a home designed by the architect Julia Morgan in Palo Alto (Fig. 67). Ornament is used sparely—only the cast iron of the balcony and the chimney top are elaborated, but the

Fig. 65: Native American, Acoma Pueblo, New Mexico.

Fig. 66: Pueblo Revival style, Sonora model home by Centex home builders, Santa Fe, New Mexico.

key features are still present: a pitched tile roof and white stucco walls. The "Spanish Style" model offered by Centex Homes in 2012 has the featured elements of a tile roof and stucco surfaces, but it uses flatter (segmental) arches instead of semicircular ones, and several roofs (Fig. 68). In the Palo Alto example, the single volume feels more

Fig. 67: Spanish Colonial Revival style, John G. Kennedy House, Julia Morgan, architect, Palo Alto, California, 1921–1922.

Fig. 68: Spanish style model home by Centex Homes, 2012.

serene than the broken-up massing of the Centex model. The latter also has shutters with curved tops and features the two-car garage on the front façade, a treatment that differs from earlier demonstrations of the style. Despite its origins, the Spanish style sometimes gets swept into larger categories that combine styles.

Fig. 69: The Last Supper, from a design by Raphael.

MINIMAL CUES

It is obvious from the comparisons above that styles have been continually transformed over the centuries, but the changes of the last seventy years have made distinct styles increasingly unrecognizable. Not only the styles but also the detailed elements by which they are identified have been transformed. What has happened to the details? Minimal cues have replaced them. **Minimal cues** are the elements, often alone or in small groups, that suggest subconsciously the idea of a style by reference to only a few parts or pieces. A minimal cue is a fragment of a whole system that has disappeared. This is an important concept, particularly among real estate agents for whom minimal cues are the sole indicators of what a style might be.

Let's look for a moment at a minimal cue for a familiar motif from history, a **triplet window** that is arched in the center and has a flat-topped window on each side. The motif appeared in imperial Roman architecture, and it was used by artists and architects in the Italian Renaissance. The famous architect Donato Bramante used it for a window treatment in the Sala Regia of the Vatican Palace in the early sixteenth century. It is known from an early sixteenth-century engraving showing

The Last Supper in front of such a window (Fig. 69). The motif, however, would probably not have become widespread unless it was published, and that's what happened to it.

The architect Sebastiano Serlio (1475–1552) studied the works of these masterful artists in the 1520s, noted the use of the windows, and included it in his seven-book treatise (published 1537–1549). His book illustrated the use of the windows in designs for grand residences (Fig. 70). As Serlio's books spread, the window's name became associated with him, so it became known as a **Serlian window,** or Serliana.

Andrea Palladio, the Italian architect I mentioned earlier, made the motif central to his designs. After he published his own treatise, *Quattro Libri dell'Architettura* (Four Books on Architecture) in 1570, the motif became well known to architects all over Europe. Subsequently, Palladio's books were so broadly published that his architecture became the most influential style throughout the world. And the **Palladian style** continues to have an impact on the images of high-end houses produced by the building industry. Palladio's use of the motif and the widespread publishing of it in his work gave him

Fig. 70: Venice Palazzo; Sebastiano Serlio, architect.

Fig. 71: Serliana motif, Simonton Windows advertisement, 2004.

much of the credit for the motif over the next four centuries. The **Palladian window** has already appeared in our examples of Colonial style architecture.

My point in this historical digression is that already by the early sixteenth-century this architectural motif had a history of use and reuse in domestic and civic architecture. The image of the Serliana has persisted with hardiness for centuries, but its meaning has changed over time. While its history has, for the most part, been long forgotten, the motif persists as a minimal cue for classical architecture. Although the motif for the window has remained the same for five centuries, the technology of the window has gone through radical changes. The Palladian window, with its sixteenth-century roots, is now created by a big commercial manufacturer that uses the latest glazing technology to produce a strong, leak-proof, energy-efficient, and long-lasting window product (Fig. 71).

NAMES AND THEMES

Relying on styles to give coherent identities to our houses may no longer be possible. The styles as they have been known for centuries are being transformed out of existence. The more we look, the more we see that stylistic categories are vanishing or are being treated as totally exchangeable, regardless of the actual house plan. This interchangeability is clear in three designs from McCaffrey Homes at the Braden Court development, a neighborhood within Loma Vista, a master-planned "urban village" in the city of Clovis, California, near Fresno. McCaffrey Homes, a family-run company in business for thirty-five years, has built over eight thousand homes, mostly throughout California's San Joaquin Valley. Their Kaitlyn model house contains two to three bedrooms, two and a half baths, and a two-car garage in 1,678 square feet. You can select it in one of three style options: French, Italian, and Craftsman (Figs. 72–74). When we compare them side by side, we see that they are the same house with minor alterations to the front façade and roof. Look closely at the French and Italian versions. The roof of the French version has a pitched, projecting gable, but is otherwise identical to the Italian. The second-story windows in the French version have a single window on the far left, instead of the pair of windows in the Italian. In the French version, the window in the bay is arched, while it is flat in the Italian version. And the shutters, which are decorative and not operable, are curved at the top in the French version and flat in the Italian model. On the first floor, the entry of the French version is flat with a beam, while the entry of the Italian version is arched, with some moldings. The Craftsman model is similar to both, but differs in its entry and has a roof gable on the side of the house. The minimal cues that identify it as Craftsman style are the brackets (L-shaped wooden elements) and the tapered columns at the entry. Aside from a couple of other very minor differences, in every other aspect all these floor plans are identical.

The use of styles that were once recognized and understood has given way to real estate agents, developers, and builders identifying houses by names and themes. It is no longer styles but names and themes that define a house. Those names provide subtle associations that operate on our memory at both a personal and a cultural level.

Naming applies not only to individual houses but also to streets, neighborhoods, and subdivisions. Let's go back and look at our visit to Circle C Ranch. Its name is literally a

Fig. 72: French style option, Kaitlyn model, 2012.

Fig. 73: Italian style option, Kaitlyn model, 2012.

Fig. 74: Craftsman style option, Kaitlyn model, 2012.

reminder that this large tract of land was formerly a ranch. Regardless of the fact that none of the houses resembles traditional ranch houses and that the land itself was covered in live oaks, junipers, and native grasses instead of broad, open expanses for grazing cattle, horses, and sheep, the name of the place connotes the old traditions of Texas. The names of streets within the subdivision do not, however, automatically follow the ranch theme. In some subdivisions, developers are hard pressed to name streets, and they may end up giving streets the names of their friends or of employees who work for the company. In the area of KB Home next to Fairway Estates, the streets are named after players and coaches of the Pittsburgh Steelers football team—somebody was a fan of the team. The names of the twelve house plans in Fairway Homes come from the names of famous golf courses: Sawgrass, Sunningdale, Hazeltine, Pinehurst, St. Andrews, Oakmont, Spyglass, Westchester, Turnberry, Pebble Beach, Augusta, and Shinnecock. If you are a golfer or a fan the game, these names may be familiar. They reflect the theme of golf as a leisure activity, which is reinforced by the fact that one side of this high-end subdivision flanks a semiprivate golf course.

En route to Fairway Estates, and before we even arrived, we saw the names of places that were intended to set a mood. Escarpment Village was on our right as we drove along the divided roads of the development. The name **"Escarpment Village"** is itself a sort of minimal cue for the Balcones Escarpment, a geological feature that runs through western Austin and is sometimes considered a marker for "where the West begins." The image of an escarpment at a village also suggests a small, intimate settlement where everyone knew everyone else and people traveled by horse and cart, in small and quaint circumstances. But there is no escapement, and this is not a village but a shopping center that is nearly identical to thousands found throughout the country. After we arrive at Fairway Estates, we don't see estates, but houses on conventional lots. The house models, which are named after golf courses, flank a golf course that can survive only thanks to extensive irrigation in a semiarid climate. Only a limited number of lots lie along the golf course, and though home owners can look at golfers moving up and down the course in their electric carts, fences, which provide security and mark property boundaries, separate them from the open expanse. The golf course is an object to be looked at, not strolled through.

The use of themes to identify houses is neither new nor a recent invention. Themes were obvious in various Sears mail-order projects, as suggested by the house model names Lexington and Elsmore. Themes are intended to add layers of association to a home and ground it, giving it a sense of identity and place. That place

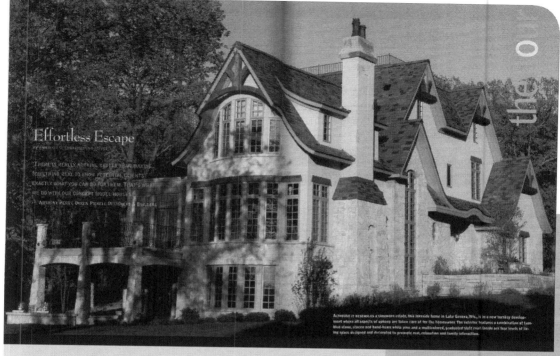

Fig. 75: "Old World European" home, Lake Geneva, Wisconsin.

is intended to call up a range of positive experiences and suggest that important needs, including security, comfort, and prestige, are being met. Theming now has become the dominant means of giving identity to homes. By contrast, styles have been either rendered meaningless or crammed into vague, general, all-encompassing categories. The expansion of theming in the building industry has risen in parallel with the idea of branding. Again, brands have been around for a long time, but the media (particularly digital media), global accessibility, and expanding markets have made branding more important than ever in the housing industry.

Themes: European Style and Mediterranean Style

One example of a major theme in housing can be seen in the **European style,** which is particularly popular now. The style's features—angled walls, columns, circular windows, double-height entries, and "true radius" (semicircular) arches—are all perceived as having high value. Nobody seems to know exactly why that is the case, but it is the perception of value that counts. An example of the dissolving of stylistic categories can be seen in a house published in *Luxury Home Builder* (September 2003), a supplement to *Professional Builder* (Fig. 75). With no mention of its neo-Tudor antecedents, the style of the home is identified as "Old World European." Since we see

the Tour

Personal Touch
BY ANN MATESI, CONTRIBUTING EDITOR

Fig. 76: Mediterranean Revival style home, Gainesville, Florida.

Europe as the Old World, the term is redundant, but it reinforces the ideas of tradition and Europe. The accompanying article, titled "Effortless Escape," explains that the house is intended to show potential clients what builders can do for them. Resembling a "timeworn estate," this waterfront home in Lake Geneva, Wisconsin, is in a new **"turnkey"** luxury development, that is, a development where everything is completed and all that the buyer has to do is turn the front-door key and move in. Described in the accompanying text as "in the tradition of the East Coast compound where family gathers with friends," the house has four interior levels of living space "designed and decorated to promote rest, relaxation and family interaction." Intended for buyers in their late forties, the 6,824-square-foot house had an estimated market value of $3.65 million.

A variation of the European theme is the **Mediterranean style.** The style can be seen in another house (Fig. 76) whose plan was published in *Luxury Home Builder*. It is part of Biltmore Estates, in Gainesville, Florida, a twenty-four-home enclave of luxury-estate-style residences . A local builder, Barry Rutenberg, provided the "flexible" floor plan, which is meant to suit a variety of home-buyer profiles—"a critical feature for a spec-built project." With 5,578 square feet, it is less expensive than the previous example, having a market value of $900,000. The difference in value may be attributable to land costs and the use of different basic materials: shingles instead of metal roofing, "Acrocrete, Cultured Stone" instead of stucco and real stone.

Fig. 77: Mediterranean Style, Napoli II house, Longwood, Florida.

But what defines the Gainesville house as Mediterranean is unclear. It includes a Palladian window, three different kinds of window tops (round, flat, and segmental), and oval windows familiar from Colonial styles.

This Mediterranean style house in Gainesville also includes a feature that is widely used not just in this category but in other models as well, the **double-height entry.** Not a standard feature of residential architecture based on classical principles, it was used, instead, in Roman architecture for **triumphal arches,** the constructions through which victorious Roman military figures would march as they paraded their conquered victims. The legacy of such use is long forgotten, but the double-height entry is widespread in the housing industry, which is why it appears several times in earlier sections. There is no clear explanation why this practice exists, but it probably is intended to create a feeling of grandeur. Because so few people enter their homes through the front door, where the tall archway is located, it acts more as a sign to visitors, neighbors, and people driving by. Grandeur aside, when the ceilings of the first floor are only a standard height of eight feet, the use of the archway going up to the second floor can appear awkward and top heavy. Consequently, the proportions associated with the grandeur and grace of historic houses are missing.

A third house in *Luxury Home Builder,* the Napoli II, was showcased in the 2003 Central Florida Parade of Homes (Fig. 77). Sized at 5,388 square feet, it is located in

Longwood, Florida, and had a market value of $1.34 million. Johnson Estate Designs of Maitland, Florida, acted as architect for the project. This home's style is also "Mediterranean," but the only Mediterranean feature, aside from its name recalling Naples, Italy, is the roof of concrete tiles, unless arched windows with fanlights flanked by columns qualify as Mediterranean.

The Napoli II uses the same kind of interior plan found in thousands of other examples, with angled circulation spines providing irregular polygonal spaces, asymmetry, and an absence of **axial movement** or **spatial progression.** If you ask why the floor plans are arranged the way they are, you may not get a direct answer. The salesperson usually has no idea who designed the house, how the design evolved, or why. The actual answers lie in behind-the-scenes decisions that reflect marketing surveys, previous selling results, and a multitude of other factors. If we ask ourselves what we feel in the interiors of these big houses, we get very personal impressions. Angled walls on the floor plans and built interiors seem to be opening outward, as if square or rectangular spaces are more confining. In reality, orderly rectilinear spaces are easier to furnish. Builders may say that "open" and "airy" are desirable or *interesting* commodities, but not in the sense of modern open space that extends without boundaries. From a builder's perspective, a preference for open interiors combines well with traditional exteriors, traditional furnishings, and columns, but with not with spatial voids or modern furniture.

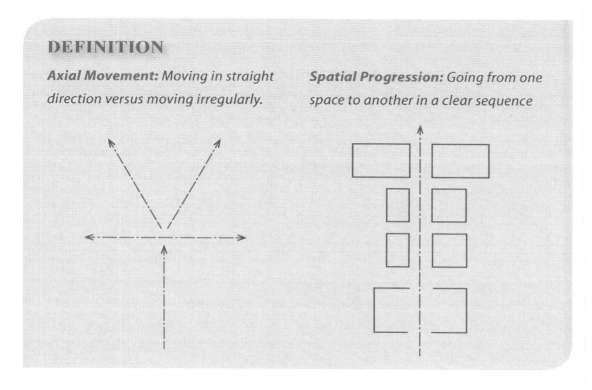

DEFINITION

Axial Movement: *Moving in straight direction versus moving irregularly.*

Spatial Progression: *Going from one space to another in a clear sequence*

These three examples of large, high-end Mediterranean houses were built before the full-scale economic downturn of 2008, but they demonstrate some fundamental themes still at work in the housing industry, and they tend to confirm that styles are dissolving. We know the themes these houses represent because the media, including television, magazines, and the Internet, tell us their names. This information is available when you visit the builder's model houses, where you meet the salespersons who will explain the house to you. You, the buyer, know the house is European style or Mediterranean style because the sales agents say so. The brochures obtained on your visits reinforce the theme concept of the house.

Although having a clear grasp of style is secondary when it comes to selling a house, the role of technology is increasingly important as a marketing tool. We are informed that the Napoli II is "Technology-Friendly." This is the high-tech house of the present. To home builders, **high-tech** means home theaters, automated lighting, and "structured wiring." Technology will allow these houses to operate automatically, with the integration of lighting, security, heating and air conditioning, and entertainment systems. Houses that light up before you come home, as well as self-adjusting landscape lighting, provide an added security feature. The promotion of a house's technology, whether its price is low, middle, or high, will become an increasingly important marketing feature in the future.

Themes: Tuscan Style

Finally, we need to look at the **Tuscan style,** a major theme throughout the housing industry (Fig. 78). Although it became popular in Southern California in the 1990s, the Tuscan style is found in so many locations throughout the country that it comes close to being a national style. The memoir *Under the Tuscan Sun* (1996), which has sold millions of copies worldwide and rhapsodized about the *dolce vita*, added to the appeal of the style. While historians have defined a Tuscan order by its rustic and stubby column (recall our discussion of true classical styles), they have not included it as a standard in conventional histories of American architecture. It is an invention that emerged as a popular style only during the last major housing boom. It evokes popular images of the Italian countryside, with red barrel-vaulted roofs and deep ochre stucco exteriors (Fig. 79). It is largely derived from the Spanish Colonial and Mission Revival styles. From whole subdivisions to one-off high-end custom homes, the focus is on a "rustic, old-world appeal" to buyers. The Tuscan style is a primary example of the influence of builder culture, semi-custom housing, and home-improvement media in the formation of composite, new architectural styles.

Fig. 78: Tuscan style, Las Palmas model home, Palm Beach Gardens, Florida.

Fig. 79: Tuscan house in La Serra, Carmignano, Tuscany.

Despite a lack of any historical grounding, the Tuscan style receives considerable attention in builder literature and on do-it-yourself television programs and websites. Devotees of the style can even find websites for Tuscan style interior design. HGTV regularly features Tuscan as an interior decoration treatment; its elements include faux finishes, wrought-iron accessories, and distressed furniture. The style can be used as a surface treatment and applied to the plain interiors of existing builder homes.

Sometimes the minimal cues of the Tuscan style are combined with other styles, but without the designer realizing the differences between the motifs. The round tower, a well-known feature in the nineteenth century, as seen an image of a **Norman style** villa published by A. J. Downing (Fig. 80), was also part of Queen Anne style architecture in the late nineteenth century, as well as an element of Spanish Revival architecture. Somehow it found its way into a house design for the Tuscan Village in Lakeway, Texas (Fig. 81). The tower itself is not particularly Tuscan, and the

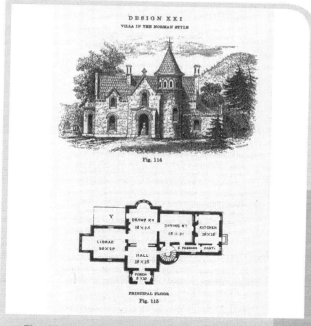

Fig. 80: Norman style villa, 19th Century.

Fig. 81: Tuscan Village advertisement, Austin, Texas, 2011.

Fig. 82: Tuscan style, Austin, Texas, 2012.

tall chimney belongs to a different style as well. This design's association with Tuscan character relies more on the roof tile than anything else. Despite the limited output of the building industry during the downturn, Tuscan-themed designs increasingly absorbed remnants of the former Classical styles, the Mediterranean style, and the Spanish Revival style (Fig. 82).

What counts in the Tuscan theme is a vague association of an idyllic lifestyle with the *dolce vita* of Italy, languishing under a grape arbor and sipping wine after having eaten a delightful pasta dish drizzled with olive oil. In Tuscany, we feel the sun and closeness of nature in an ancient landscape. It all sounds very appealing. And this may indeed be the theme you want to characterize your lifestyle. It may remind you of a lovely vacation in Italy. On the other hand, do we prefer images reminiscent of Italy because American building culture—in either traditional or modern styles—provides no satisfactory alternative? 🏠

Making Choices

Once you visit some of today's subdivisions and compare their homes to housing from the past, you will see that our building stock on the whole is probably better built now than at any time before. Even at the low end of the price spectrum, the quality of our homes and the materials used in them are constantly improving. Looking at mass-produced homes as a total package, American consumers get great value for their money. There are few places in the world where so many people can quickly obtain good shelter for their families in a detached house sitting on a bit of land at such reasonable prices.

The housing industry is constantly incorporating new technology into its products. It is also becoming more **energy conscious** and has begun to build in new ways with innovative materials and new systems that save energy. I think that in the future this conserving tendency, and other so-called green applications, will be applied to the use of water and wastewater as well as electricity. The housing industry is already moving in this direction because green features are now selling points, and every point counts in such a highly competitive field.

We have seen that the evolution of construction methods, materials, and new technologies constantly moves forward, but these developments are independent of changes in how a house looks. Everything under the building's skin is evolving, but the surface image has no connection to those changes. The building industry spends less on design than on any other item budgeted for the production of a house. In other words, technology will always be there and always evolve, but it is not necessarily in sync with the style or theme of a home. Our technology comes from the twenty-first century, but the images of "home" generally come from the nineteenth century or even earlier (Fig. 83). Sometimes the past still calls to us, as we have seen in the enduring attraction of Palladio's villas.

From the building industry's perspective, the look of a home is only important as a feature in marketing. All its pieces and parts—from granite counters to crown moldings—are, we are told, the things that make a house valuable. Very few care about its character, proportions, or siting as fundamentals that will affect your long-term enjoyment and determine whether the house reflects a style or not. What matters is what sells, and if a product is successful, its formula for success is repeated.

What's wrong with this picture? On one hand, nothing. Successful selling is the goal of the work that most of us do. It is a prime value in our society and the means of our sustenance. On the other hand, a **home** is something more than a consumer item with a brief life, to be used and then tossed out. A home is not the same sort of object as a car you trade in every few years. But our grasp of a home's importance has gradually softened. Americans have always been highly mobile, first moving across the continent from one coast to another, then getting in the habit of changing houses with almost the same frequency of changing cars. The typical suburban dweller lives in a house for seven years and then plans to move elsewhere. But under the current economic scenario—both in America and around the globe— it appears most of us are in for leaner financial times over the long term, and that has already affected people's lifestyles. Young people are marrying later and having families later. Single adult children are living with their parents in the homes they grew up in, something that was unimaginable twenty years ago. And people who worry about their job security and retirement funds may make their housing choices more carefully, with the result that they may move less often and stay longer where they first buy. Under these conditions, the feel of your home, its look, and its ability to provide comfort are more important than ever.

Here's where we get back to the **issue of identity.** Your home represents who you are. This is a good thing. If you want to imagine living in Tuscany while you reside in Scottsdale, Arizona, then you have made a choice, and I'd love to share a plate of ravioli with you in a place you enjoy. But the important thing is to have made a choice. To choose well, you need to be aware: Does the home you are considering

Fig. 83: Impasse Termite Blocker, advertisement.

really represent who you are and what you think is a genuine depiction of what you want? Is it an image that is passing or timeless? **Answering these questions can help your dream home become a reality.**

I had lunch with a friend, a brilliant writer and expert on homes, and we talked about these issues. He insisted that what housing looks like is largely controlled by the housing industry. The industry offers the products, you select from those offerings, and you have no other choices beyond the existing house stock. I disagree, and I have been implying throughout this book that you, as an educated consumer, can inform the building industry more effectively than ever. But if the public doesn't know what to ask for or how to evaluate what is being offered in a tract house, things won't change. People can't ask for what they don't know about. The building industry wants to know what you want, which is why it constantly surveys people. If consumers are savvy and speak out, the market will respond.

To be a better, savvier home buyer and get more bang for your buck, you need to:

- **learn about the process of making and marketing houses**
- **understand how selecting options for your home is a major cost factor**
- **consider the impact of styles and themes on the identity of your home**
- **communicate what you want and don't automatically accept what you are offered**

This book has been attempt to give you more knowledge, more confidence, and better control in the buying or building of your dream home. 🏠

SOURCES

The following references are a few suggestions for further reading and may be helpful in your preparations to buy or build your dream home.

Online Sources

Websites, by their digital natures, tend to be transient, so any recommendations here are subject to change. Furthermore, the proliferation of web sources can be overwhelming. Some places to look before you start a search:

HUD Home Buying Guide: A free government document that describes the process of buying a home under U.S. Department of Housing and Urban Development guidelines:
> http://portal.hud.gov/hudportal/documents/huddoc?id=DOC_12163.pdf

National Association of Home Builders website: http://www.nahb.com/

National Association of Realtors website: http://www.realtor.org/

Housingzone.com is the online hub to multiple building trade magazines:
> *Professional Builder* (http://www.housingzone.com/professionalbuilder),
> *Professional Remodeler* (http://www.housingzone.com/professionalremodeler),
> *Custom Builder* (http://www.housingzone.com/custombuilder).

For general advice, *Consumer Reports,* the long-standing independent publication, provides
> helpful assessments of products. See www.ConsumerReports.org.

Sources in Other Languages

Non-English-language sources should expand to facilitate the broadening base of the American home buyer.

For a good Spanish language portal to a broad range of subjects published by the US Department of Housing and Urban Development, see *Viviendas y Comunidades* at http://espanol.hud.gov/home.html.

Spanish language newspapers, such as *Reforma* and *El Norte,* may also be helpful sources.

Shelter Magazines

Shelter magazines are still numerous, but with the ongoing transfer of print media to digital formats, their days may be limited. And with fewer magazines, home buyers will increasing turn to the Internet for the pictures of their dream homes. Here are a few magazines (with their start dates) to consider while they are still in print.

House Beautiful (1896)
Architectural Digest (1920)
Better Homes and Gardens (1922)
Southern Living (1966)
Country Living (1978)
Midwest Living (1987)
Veranda (1987)
Traditional Home (1989)
Elle Décor (1989)
Martha Stewart Living (1990)

This Old House (1995)
Dwell (2000)
Real Simple (2000)
Lonny (2009)
Nesting Newbies (2009)
Pure Green Living Magazine (2010)
Rue Magazine (2010)
Matchbook: Field Guide to a Charmed Life (2011)
High Gloss (2011)
HGTV Magazine (2011)

Style Guides

Although we have seen that styles have given way to themes as the driving force in design, you may enjoy knowing more about the major styles as they used to be present in the history of American architecture. Such knowledge will also help you understand more about what your new home is and is not.

Books:

Baker, John Milnes. *American House Styles: A Concise Guide.* New York: Norton, 1994.

Blumenson, John J. G. *Identifying American Architecture: A Pictorial Guide to Styles and Terms, 1600–1945.* New York: Norton, 1981.

Foster, Gerald L. *American Houses: A Field Guide to the Architecture of the Home.* Boston: Houghton Mifflin, 2004.

Hayden, Dolores, and Jim Wark. *A Field Guide to Sprawl.* New York: Norton, 2004.

Ierley, Merritt. *Open House: A Guided Tour of the American Home, 1637–Present.* New York: Holt, 1999.

Massey, James, and Shirley Maxwell. *House Styles in America: The Old-House Journal Guide to the Architecture of American Homes.* New York: Penguin Studio, 1996.

McAlester, Virginia. *Great American Houses and Their Architectural Styles.* New York: Abbeville, 1994.

McAlester, Virginia, and Lee McAlester. *A Field Guide to American Houses.* New York: Knopf, 1984.

Morgan, William. *The Abrams Guide to American House Styles.* New York: Abrams, 2004.

Pickering, Earnest. *The Homes of America as They Have Expressed the Lives of Our People for Three Centuries.* New York: Crowell, 1951.

Poppeliers, John C., and S. Allen Chambers, Jr. *What Style Is It? A Guide to American Architecture.* New York: Wiley, 2003.

Walker, Les. *American Shelter: An Illustrated Encyclopedia of the American Home.* Woodstock, N.Y.: Overlook, 1981.

Online Style Guides:

http://www.realtor.com/home-garden/home-styles/

http://www.frontdoor.com/buy/home-styles-guide-features-and-examples-of-residential architecture/1088

http://realtormag.realtor.org/home-and-design/guide-residential-styles

http://www.newalbanypreservation.com/uploads/File/designguidelines/NAguides-stylesres.pdf

Handbooks on Buying and Building:

This selection focuses on specific questions you may have; the books cover topics ranging from remodeling to buying a new home.

Abram, Norm. *Ask Norm: 250 Answers to Questions about your Home from Television's Foremost Home Improvement Expert.* New York: This Old House Books, 2001.

Connolly, William G. *The New York Times Guide to Buying or Building a Home.* New York: Times Books, 1984.

Cummins, Martin. *Designing and Building Your Own Home.* Ramsbury, UK: Crowood, 2006.

Fields, Alan, and Denise Fields. *Your New House: The Alert Consumer's Guide to Buying and Building a Quality Home.* Boulder, Colo.: Windsor Peak, 2002.

Heberle, David, and Richard Scutella. *How to Plan, Contract, and Build Your Own Home.* New York: McGraw-Hill Professional Books, 2000.

Locke, James. *The Well-Built House.* New York: Houghton Mifflin Harcourt, 1988, 1992.

Nash, George. *Do-It-Yourself Housebuilding: The Complete Handbook.* New York: Sterling, 1995.

Salant, Katherine. *The Brand-New House Book: Everything You Need to Know About Planning, Designing, and Building a Custom, Semi-Custom, or Production-Built House.* New York: Three Rivers Press, 2001.

Architects

If you don't want to enter the housing market through its commercially produced subdivisions or don't want to buy a builder's spec house, then you might consider hiring an architect for a true custom-designed home. Repetition allows production builders to charge low prices; unique houses by architects are a different matter. My colleague Witold Rybczynski compared selling prices for the same home built on the same lot. As constructed by NVR, the big national company, the house cost $299,000; by a custom builder, $495,500. An architect-designed home of the same size cost $825,350. If you do consider hiring an architect, it will be helpful to understand more about what an architect does. Many architects, including the young generation emerging from architecture schools, have a broad sense of serving the public. An architect can, in principle, provide a house that is truly designed for your specific needs, well sited, and environmentally sensitive. The process may take longer, since the design and development phase for custom work requires more time, but a skillful and careful architect can control costs and work within budgets to provide more value for each dollar spent than is found in buying a house from a building company.

Baker, John Milnes. *How to Build a House with an Architect.* Philadelphia: Lippincott, 1977.

Box, Hal. *Think Like an Architect.* Austin: University of Texas Press, 2007.

Collier, Stephen F. *Raising the Rafters: How to Work with Architects, Contractors, Interior Designers, Suppliers, Engineers, and Bankers to Get Your Dream House Built.* Woodstock, N.Y.: Overlook, 1993.

Hirsch, William J. *Designing your Perfect House: Lessons from an Architect.* Cary, N.C.: Dalsimer, 2008.

Morosco, Gerald, and Edward Massery. *How to Work with an Architect.* Layton, Utah: Gibbs Smith, 2006

Popular Books

Some insightful and talented writers have written engaging accounts of houses and homes. These complement a huge number of picture books, many of which focus exclusively on high-end houses.

The American House. London: Phaidon, 2008.

Bahamón, Alejandro. *Mini House.* New York: LOFT and Harper Design International, 2003.

Baxandall, Rosalyn, and Elizabeth Ewen. *Picture Windows: How the Suburbs Happened.* New York: Basic Books, 2000.

Berke, Deborah, and Steven Harris, eds. *Architecture of the Everyday.* New York: Princeton Architectural Press, 1997.

Bryson, Bill. *At Home: A Short History of Private Life.* New York: Doubleday, 2010.

Davis, Sam. *The Architecture of Affordable Housing.* Berkeley and Los Angeles: University of California Press, 1995.

De Valle, Cristina. *Compact Houses.* New York: Universe, 2005.

Doubilet, Susan, and Daralice Bowls. *American House Now: Contemporary Architectural Directions.* New York: Universe, 2002.

Gauer, James, and Catherine Tighe. *The New American Dream: Living Well in Small Homes.* New York: Monacelli, 2004.

Kidder, Tracy. *House.* Boston: Houghton Mifflin Harcourt, 1985, 1999.

————. *Home Town.* New York: Random House, 1999.

Low, Setha. *Behind the Gates: Life, Security, and the Pursuit of Happiness in Fortress America.* New York: Routledge, 2005.

MacDonald, Donald. *Democratic Architecture: Practical Solutions to Today's Housing Crisis.* New York: Whitney Library of Design, 1996.

Maddex, Diane, and Alexander Vertikoff. *Bungalow Nation.* New York: Abrams, 2003.

Moore, Charles, Gerald Allen, and Donlyn Lyndon. *The Place of Houses.* Berkeley and Los Angeles: University of California Press, 1974.

Moore, Charles, and Kent C. Bloomer. *Body, Memory, and Architecture.* New Haven, Conn.: Yale University Press, 1977.

Penick, Monica. "Framing Modern: Maynard L. Parker, Elizabeth Gordon, and House Beautiful's Pace Setter Program." In *Maynard L. Parker: Modern Photography and the American Dream,* ed. Jennifer A. Watts. New Haven, Conn.: Yale University Press, 2012.

Rybczynski, Witold. *Home: A Short History of an Idea.* New York: Viking, 1986.

————. *The Most Beautiful House in the World.* New York: Viking, 1989.

————. *Last Harvest: How a Cornfield became New Dalefield.* New York: Scribner, 2007.

Smith, Courtenay, and Sean Topham. *Xtreme Houses.* Munich: Prestel, 2002.

Susanka, Sarah. *Creating the Not So Big House: Insights and Ideas for the New American Home.* Newtown, Conn.: Taunton, 2000.

————. *Home by Design: Transforming Your House into Home.* Newton, Conn.: Taunton, 2004.

Susanka, Sarah, and Kira Oblensky. *The Not So Big House: A Blueprint for the Way We Live.* Newtown, Conn.: Taunton, 2008 (1998).

Waldie, D. J. *Holy Land: A Suburban Memoir.* New York: St. Martin's, 1997.

Histories

Many good histories of architecture provide broad coverage of the subject, including social issues and problems such as sprawl. In addition to books, essays and articles may contain interesting, if detailed, material on homes and housing.

Archer, John. *Architecture and Suburbia: From English Villa to American Dream House, 1690–2000.* Minneapolis: University of Minnesota Press, 2005.

Bruegmann, Robert. *Sprawl: A Compact History.* Chicago: University of Chicago, 2005.

Gutfreund, Owen D. *Twentieth Century Sprawl: Highways and the Reshaping of the American Landscape.* New York: Oxford University Press, 2004.

Handlin, David P. *The American Home: Architecture and Society, 1815–1915.* Boston: Little, Brown, 1979.

Harris, Dianne. "Screening Identity: Race, Class, and Privacy in the Ordinary Postwar House." In *Race and Landscape in America,* ed. Richard Schein. New York: Routledge, 2006.

————. *Second Suburb: Levittown, Pennsylvania.* Pittsburgh: University of Pittsburg Press, 2010.

Hayden, Dolores. *Building Suburbia: Green Fields and Urban Growth, 1820–2000*. New York: Vintage, 2004.

———. *A Grand Domestic Revolution: A History of Feminist Designs for American Homes, Neighborhoods, and Cities*. Cambridge, Mass.: MIT Press, 1981.

———. *Redesigning the American Dream: The Future of Housing, Work, and Family Life*. New York: Norton, 1984.

Hunter, Christine. *Ranches, Rowhouses, and Railroad Flats: American Homes; How They Shape Our Landscapes and Neighborhoods*. New York: Norton, 1999.

Isenstadt, Sandy. *The Modern American House: Spaciousness and Middle Class Identity*. Cambridge: Cambridge University Press, 2006.

Jackson, Kenneth T. *Crabgrass Frontier: The Suburbanization of the United States*. New York: Oxford University Press, 1985.

Kelly, Barbara M. *Expanding the American Dream: Building and Rebuilding Levittown*. Albany: State University of New York Press, 1993.

Reiff, Daniel D. *Houses from Books: Treatises, Pattern Books, and Catalogs in American Architecture, 1738–1950; A History and Guide*. University Park: Pennsylvania State University Press, 2000.

Rome, Adam. *The Bulldozer in the Countryside: Suburban Sprawl and the Rise of American Environmentalism*. Cambridge: Cambridge University Press, 2001.

Wright, Gwendolyn. *Building the Dream: A Social History of Housing in America*. New York: Pantheon, 1981.

Interior Decoration

An awareness of interior design and decoration is essential for the creation of your dream home. The subject is huge, but the following sources can provide a good start.

Becker, Holly, and Joanna Copestick. *Decorate: 1,000 Design Ideas for Everyone Room in Your Home*. San Francisco: Chronicle Books, 2011.

Carter, Darryl. *The Collected Home: Rooms with Style, Grace, and History*. New York: Random House, 2012.

Hampton, Alexa. *The Language of Interior Design*. New York: Random House, 2010.

Needleman, Deborah, Sara Costello, and Dara Caponigro. *Domino: The Book of Decorating: A Room-by-Room Guide to Creating a Home That Makes You Happy*. New York: Simon & Schuster, 2008.

Pile, John. *Color in Interior Design*. New York: McGraw-Hill, 1997.

———. *A History of Interior Design*. London: Laurence King, 2005.

Schafer, Gil. *The Great American Home: Tradition for the Way We Live Now*. New York: Rizzoli, 2012.

Thibaut-Pomerantz, Carolle. *Wallpaper: A History of Style and Trends*. Paris: Flammarion Paris, 2009.

Whiton, Augustus Sherrill, and Stanley Abercrombie. *Interior Design and Decoration*. Upper Saddle River, N.J.: Prentice Hall, 2002.

E-books

Derembert, Thomas, and Janet Handcock. *Home Interior Design Made Easy*. 2012.

NOTES

P. 25. "In a boom year like 2003…." *Professional Builder* (September 2003), p. 36.

P. 27. "While the biggest companies may generate plans from their in-house designers…" This material comes from an interview with Sarah Morrison (December 22, 2003 Washington DC) conducted by Anthony Alofsin. Sarah received a bachelor's of architecture degree from Lehigh University where she also was a business student. She worked for JWH homes (Weiland) homes in Atlanta; the job paid much more than an 'architect'.

P. 141. "Devotees of the style can even find websites for Tuscan style interior design." See http://www.tuscan-home-101.com/ My discussion of the Tuscan style draws on the research notes of Lauren G. Hamer, my assistant.

P. 149. "An architect-designed home …" Personal communication, Witold Rybczynski to author, 19 February 2013.

ACKNOWLEDGMENTS

My original research began at the Center for Advanced Studies in the Visual Arts, the research wing of the National Gallery of Art, Washington, D.C., where I was appointed the Ailsa Mellon Bruce Senior Fellow. I thank CASVA for its support and collegiality. During the Washington phase of research, I benefited from interviews with Rudy Djabbarzadeh, Judith Lanius, Sarah Morrison, and the late Robert Duemling and Louisa Duemling. Portions of the text were subsequently written with help from fellowships at the MacDowell Colony and the Helen Riaboff Whiteley Center, Friday Harbor, Washington. My friends Wheelock Whitney and Sandro Cagnin provided lodging in New York during the final writing of the book in the summer of 2012. The heart of Gotham was an ideal location to write about distant suburbs. Throughout my research and writing, I received generous ongoing support from the University of Texas at Austin through Faculty Research Assignments, the Roland Gommel Roessner Professorship in Architecture, and a Faculty Research and Project Support Grant.

I thank a talented team of young scholars and emerging practitioners who provided assistance during the research, writing, and production of the book. Samuel Dodd played a vital role in editing the text, preparing illustrations, and contributing his expertise in culture and media. Priyanka Sen provided the final coordination of the content of the book with skill, efficiency, and good cheer. Her suggestions made this a better book. Jeanie Fan transformed the text and pictures into a dynamic publication. In an earlier research phase, Lauren G. Hamer investigated the home industry as a University Research Intern Fellow. I also thank my students who visited numerous sites with me and provided their own insights on housing. Numerous other individuals provided assistance during the assembling of illustrations: Amy Stewart, Elizabeth Schaub, Erica Kelly at the Library of Congress, Kathryn Millan, and Kathryn Pierce Meyer. The sidebar studies were written by Sam Dodd (Parade of Homes) and Priyanka Sen (Wallpaper, Joseph Eichler, and Usonian Homes).

Members of the home-building industry shared their insights, knowledge, and generosity in providing permission to use their images and websites. I thank Cristy Bloomingdale; Louis and Susan Jauregui; Eric O'Malley; Mayra Perales at KB Home, the offsite sales counselor for the Central Texas region; William Allin Storer; David Walsh; and many others whom I have tried to acknowledge in the text wherever possible. Several astute readers provided feedback on drafts of the book: Minnie Hollyman, Alicia Loving, Katherine Reagan; Monika Suhnholz; Helen Thompson; and Tom Whatley. Witold Rybczynski, an articulate expert on the American home, shared his insights about the American housing industry and made helpful suggestions during the writing and editing of the text. Burnes Hollyman generously lent his expertise in digital publishing and inspired the entire venture.

Finally, I thank my wife, Patricia, who gave me the space to write *Dream Home*. She remains my prized critic in residence.

CREDITS

Every effort has been made to contact permission holders of images for each of the images in this text.

Alofsin, Anthony, 12 (2003), 13 (2012), 25–29 (2012), 32 (2010), 47, 42–43; Bennet, Mark, 14 (1986, Mark Moore Gallery); Callahan, Brian, 61 (2011); Centex Homes (2012), 70, 72; Denver Public Library, McClure Collection, 56 (photographer, L. C. McClure, 1900); Dodd, Samuel, 60, 87; Downing, Andrew Jackson, 80 (The Architecture of Country Houses, New York: Appleton, 1850); Engel, Hans, 48; E-Plans, 54; Fan, Jeanie, 9, 30 (after EcoWho www.ecowho.com/articles/6/The_importance_of_building_orientation.html, 2013), 31 (modeled after G. Z. Brown and Mark DeKay, Sun, Wind, and Light: Architectural Design Strategies, 2nd ed., p. 20); Fuller, Stephen, 10 (www.stephenfuller.com, 2012); Great Properties, vol. 3, p. 20, 15; Hathorn, Billy, 52 (2011); KB Homes (2010), 16–18, 22–24; Keller Williams, 8 ("Loyalty, That's Our Motto" advertisement); Library of Congress, 46 (Reproduction No. HABS IOWA, 77-DESMO, 6-11), 50 (photographer, Laurence E. Tilley, 1958, Reproduction No. HABS RI,4-PROV, 138-1), 54 (W. S. Stewart, photographer, 1936, Reproduction No. HABS DEL, 2-NEWCA,9-6), 55 (Carol Highsmith, photographer, The George F. Landegger Collection of Alabama Photographs in the Carol M. Highsmith's America Collection), 58 (Theodor Horydczak Collection, Reproduction No. LC-H814-T-2387-084), 63 (Carol Highsmith, photographer, The George F. Landegger Collection of Alabama Photographs), 66 (The porch was probably originally open but enclosed in this view, Reproduction No. HABS IOWA, 77-DESMO,10-1, 68, Reproduction No. HABS GA, 157-DALT,1-1), 69 (Casa Blanca vicinity, M. James Slack, photographer, 1934, Reproduction No. HABS NM, 31-ACOMP,1-52), 71 (Reproduction No. HABS CAL, 43-PALAL,3-1); Luxury Home Builder, 79 (September 2003, pp. 18–19), 80 (September 2003, pp. 36–37), 81 (September 2003, pp. 26–27); Magbee, D. Jarret, 44, © The Garlinghouse Company; McCaffrey Homes, Clovis, California, 2012, 76–78; © McGrath, Norman, 3; Palladio, Andrea, 34; Pickering, Ernest, 48 (The Homes of America As They Have Expressed the Lives of Our people for Three Centuries, New York: Crowell, 1951, p. 74, figs. 4–5); Pinnacle, vol. 32, p. 10, 62; Professional Builder, 88, Impasse Termite Blocker advertisement; Pulte Homes 2012, 67; Ryan Homes 2012, 35–43; Raimondi, Marcantonio, 73; San Antonio Express-News (Sunday, May 13, 2012) 1 (D1), 2 (D8); Sears, Roebuck and Company, 57 (1929), 65 (1916); Sen, Priyanka, 6, July 2012 Professional Builder, 7, 45 (2007); Serlio, Sebastiano, 74 (Di Architettura, Book 4 (Venice, Italy): 1587, page 9 recto, pl. 36); Simonton Windows, 75 (2004); Stewart, Amy, 19–21, 33; Thresher, Comfort (1986), 4–5; Tuscan-Harvey Homes (2007), 77–78; Tuscan Village Lakeway, Texas (2011), 81; University of Washington Special Collections, 51 (NA 2947).

26385625R00082

Made in the USA
Lexington, KY
05 October 2013